GREAT WAR

SWINDON

Remembering 1914–18

MIKE PRINGLE

The History Press

First published 2014

The History Press
The Mill, Brimscombe Port
Stroud, Gloucestershire, GL5 2QG
www.thehistorypress.co.uk

British Library Cataloguing in Publication Data.
A catalogue record for this book is available from the British Library.

ISBN 978 0 7509 5610 9

Typesetting and origination by The History Press
Printed in Great Britain

CONTENTS

TIMELINE

1914

28 June 1914

Assassination of Archduke Franz Ferdinand in Sarajevo

4 August 1914

Great Britain declares war on Germany

GWR Works' steam-hooter in Swindon announces the start of war

23 August 1914

Battle of Tannenberg commences

5 September 1914

William George becomes first Swindon man killed in action

6 September 1914

First Battle of the Marne

19 October 1914

First Battle of Ypres

1915

25 April 1915

Allied landing at Gallipoli

7 May 1915

Germans torpedo and sink the Lusitania

31 May 1915

First German Zeppelin raid on London

28 August 1915

Belgian 'Flag-Day' fete held in Town Gardens, Swindon

23 September 1915

Swindonians of 2nd Wilts march to face the Battle of Loos

20 December 1915

Allies finish their evacuation of and withdrawal from Gallipoli

26 December 1915

Swindon beat Reading 4–2 in Boxing Day football match

1916

24 January 1916

The British Government introduces conscription

21 February 1916

Battle of Verdun commences

First tribunal in Swindon to determine those excused from service

31 May 1916

Battle of Jutland

4 June 1916

Brusilov Offensive commences

5 June 1916

Swindonians lost along with Lord Kitchener on HMS Hampshire

1 July 1916

First day of the Battle of the Somme with 57,000 British casualties

27 August 1916

Italy declares war on Germany

18 December 1916

Battle of Verdun ends

1917

5 April 1917

William Gosling from Swindon awarded Victoria Cross for defusing a mortar shell

6 April 1917

The United States declares war on Germany

9 April 1917

Battle of Arras

24 April 1917

Ten Swindonians vanish without trace at 'Swindon Hill' in Macedonia

31 July 1917

Third Battle of Ypres (Passchendaele)

20 August 1917

Third Battle of Verdun

26 October 1917

Second Battle of Passchendaele

20 November 1917

Battle of Cambrai

7 December 1917

USA declares war on Austria-Hungary

1918

29 January 1918

Ration cards issued to every house in Swindon

3 March 1918

Russia and the Central Powers sign the Treaty of Brest-Litovsk

21 March 1918

Second Battle of the Somme

200 Swindon men taken prisoner on a single day

15 July 1918

Second Battle of the Marne

8 August 1918

Battle of Amiens, first stage of the Hundred Days Offensive

22 September 1918

The Great Allied Balkan victory

27 September 1918

Storming of the Hindenburg Line

8 November 1918

Armistice negotiations commence

9 November 1918

Kaiser Wilhelm II abdicates, Germany is declared a Republic

11 November 1918

Armistice Day, cessation of hostilities on the Western Front

Swindon schoolchildren told to go home for celebrations

ACKNOWLEDGEMENTS

This book could not have been written without the help and advice of many people. In particular, thanks must go to Mark Sutton, Swindon's leading Great War authority, whose enthusiasm, breadth of knowledge, and vast collection of images and ephemera about Swindon's fighting men have been invaluable. Thanks are also due to Frances Bevan and Katherine Cole, and the other staff of Swindon's Local Studies Library, as well as all those others whose research and works have provided invaluable sources of information. Finally, a huge debt of gratitude is due to W.D. Bavin and his remarkable record of events, *Swindon's War Record*, the definitive description of Swindon's Great War, published in 1922. This book is simply a retelling of the story Bavin captured while the war was tearing down lives around him a century ago. Unattributed quotes in the book are words/phrases from Bavin's book.

All period photographs used with kind permission from the collections of Mark Sutton, the Swindon Society (courtesy of Bob Townsend), and newspapers of the time (*Swindon Advertiser* and *North Wilts Herald*, thanks to the *Swindon Advertiser* and Swindon Local Studies Library).

Maps and extra photography by the author, except Mary Slade's OBE, photograph by Frances Bevan, with thanks to the Wiltshire & Swindon History Centre, Chippenham. Period artefacts are courtesy of Mark Sutton and information relating to Purton is courtesy of Bob Lloyd.

INTRODUCTION

In the early 1800s Swindon was little more than an agricultural village perched on the top of a hill surrounded by the tranquil beauty of the Wiltshire countryside. It had a population of less than 2,000, two main streets, a cattle market and the requisite number of inns. All of that changed with the Industrial Revolution, first with the arrival of the canals and then, in 1841, when Isambard Kingdom Brunel decided to site the colossal Works of the Great Western Railway (GWR) near the base of the hill.

At the advent of the Great War in 1914, the town had grown to a population of over 60,000, with all the developments and amenities that such a bustling population demands. Along with the GWR was also the Midland & South West Junction (M&SWJ) railway, making it the perfect place to help troops get from one end of the country to the other. At that time, the GWR Works employed over 10,000 people, making it one of the largest industrial centres the country had ever known. To give a simple illustration of the scale: over the four years of the war, the Swindon Works were a major contributor to the GWR's production of an astonishing 216,350 vehicles, from locomotives and ambulance trains, to open-sided horse wagons and water carts. In addition, the workers of Swindon turned out 250,000 artillery shells, nearly 500,000 fuses, 5 million cartridge cases, countless weapon components, many guns (anti-aircraft guns, 4.5in howitzers, 60-pounders) and even some large naval artillery pieces.

Partly because of the nation's need for the sort of heavy engineering the GWR could provide, Swindon initially prospered during the war, with employment high and many smaller companies doing well too. The Imperial Tobacco Company's factory (owned by W.D. & H.O. Wills) was taken over for munitions, and another factory opened up for the manufacture of rope and sails, employing fifty girls. Meanwhile, McIlroy's department store won an order from the War Office to produce 45,000 beds. Things changed, however, as the war dragged on, and Swindon suffered along with the rest of the country. As well as coping with over 5,000 men away at war (10 per cent of the population, of whom some 1,300 never came home again), the people endured the hardships of incomes going down and food controls going up through 1917; the crippling rationing of food, fuel and just about every other necessity became part of a daily struggle by 1918. Nonetheless, the resilience and generosity of the town's people, and their commitment to local industry and their society, carried Swindon through.

The scale and global importance of Swindon's GWR Works have led it to being called the 'Cape Canaveral' of its time.

This book is in honour of the people of Swindon, and the sacrifices they made. It commemorates those who endured the horrors of war, whether their part was played in the mud and shells of Flanders, or in the vast support network behind the lines. The book also celebrates the countless unnamed individuals who were left behind and, through their own heroic efforts, kept the 'home fires burning', providing direct and indirect help throughout the four years of conflict, ensuring a stable future for those who returned, their families and their descendants.

In 1918 the local council commissioned W.D. Bavin to compile a record of Swindon's activity throughout the war. Bavin noted that:

It may possibly strike some that much of the substance of this work is trivial – 'the rustic cackle of our bourg' – without interest beyond the limits of Swindon. But the sketch of the civil life of a large community during such a momentous period as that through which we have passed is not trivial, and if such an account could be found for some town of England during one of the Great Wars of the Plantagenets every detail would be prized by historians.

This book, nearly 100 years later, is written in the same spirit.

1

OUTBREAK OF WAR

At 7.40 p.m. on Tuesday, 4 August 1914, the hooter at the Great Western Railway (GWR) Works in Swindon gave out ten mighty blasts to announce that Britain was at war. The town that responded was a booming, modern centre of industrial power and success, dominated by the Great Western Railway's massive Works since 1841. But that was not the whole picture of life in this Wiltshire town as the country went to war.

National Crossroads

Swindon is a place where roads meet: a place of connectivity and access by virtue of its geographical location. The southern approach to Swindon is dominated by two Iron Age hill forts, at Barbury and Liddington, overlooking a gap in the chalk hills of the North Wessex Downs and the country's oldest road, the prehistoric Ridgeway. Perhaps unsurprisingly, given that Swindon is firmly situated in the ancient Wiltshire landscape that includes Stonehenge and Avebury, the connections to that prehistoric world are strong. As well as Bronze Age round barrows, there is even a small stone circle on the southern side of Swindon, on Day House Lane. When the Romans arrived, the geographical location was again capitalised on for connecting different parts of the country and two major roads were built amid a rich area of settlement. Like their prehistoric forebears, the Romans utilised the land for agriculture, with abundant trees for wood, clay and stone for ceramics and building, and grasslands that were ideal for raising cattle. After being mentioned in Domesday Book, the place continued to grow, sometimes sporadically, through the medieval period, eventually achieving a market charter in 1626. Benefitting from the dreadful effects of plague elsewhere, and the growth in fame of its local Purbeck Limestone, Swindon prospered in the seventeenth and eighteenth centuries and developed into a small, well thought of country town. In the early 1800s, the town again benefitted from its geography, being an ideal place for canals to pass through, connecting it to new places and creating opportunities for the burgeoning quarry industry. Then, as the Industrial Revolution really got under way, that same geography made Swindon the ideal choice for the railways, and, in 1841, Brunel decided to site the colossal Works of the GWR nearby. Indeed, the connectivity of the place has remained strong, with rail and the M4 now connecting east and west, and the A419 joining Swindon to the M5 and M6, connecting north and south-west. Being such a confluence, it is perhaps no surprise that Swindon is famous today for its Magic Roundabout. And, as mentioned in the Introduction, it was this facet of Swindon that made it so important at the outset of the war in 1914.

A Tale of Two Towns

In the first fifty years after Brunel and Daniel Gooch set up the GWR Works, the combined population of the original Swindon, plus the industry-focused new area, grew from under 5,000 to over 45,000 – a growth of 822 per cent. The national figure for growth over that time was about 80 per cent, while for Wiltshire there was a dip in population, down 8 per cent, perhaps partly due to people moving to the work available in Swindon. However, Swindon was no longer the 'Old Town' that it had been, rather it was dominated by the 'New Town' that had sprung up to support the GWR Works. And the relationship between these two towns had never been a comfortable one. When the GWR first put forward their plans to site the Works at Swindon, they were hoping to build right at the foot of the hill on which the original town was sited.

At the outset of the war, the GWR Works was very much in its heyday with non-stop production of locomotives.

This would have given them closer access to the town, its people and its facilities. Unfortunately for Brunel and Gooch, the plans were squashed by objections from the local lords of the manor, the Goddard family. As a result, the Works were built 2 miles further north, and with the new location came a need to provide facilities and housing for the enormous numbers of employees required. It was not until 1900 that the two towns actually started co-operating with each other, with houses and side streets being built along Victoria Road, creating a real link between the two areas and the forming of a single municipal borough.

Driven by Steam

In the early years of the new unified Swindon, life was not always easy, even before the war arrived. The period followed the severe national depression of the 1880s and early 1890s, which had an adverse effect on Swindon, particularly because of the town's dependence on the railway industry, as demand for rail travel inevitably fell. Outside the town, the all-important agricultural economy was also affected by the depression and by the developments of the Industrial Revolution. On the positive side, the Industrial Revolution also brought new, different employment in the form of quarrying and canals, with the canals also providing cheaper coal from places like the Welsh coalfields. This was beneficial for individuals and businesses alike. And, even after the two towns had officially joined, the GWR was still by far the biggest employer, overwhelming the agriculture which had previously been such a mainstay of the area's industry. Fortunately for Swindon, the GWR came out of the depression well, having focused much of its effort on the Swindon Works in tough times, rather than spreading itself too thinly over all the GWR sites across the country. The company worked on making improvements to the way they built locomotives and carriages, meaning that as business picked up again the Swindon site was poised to lead the railway industry, delivering ever higher standards in safety, comfort and rail technology.

In the years leading up to the war, GWR's success created more jobs, and fuelled other industries locally, such as the many retail and service industries needed to provide for the growing population. The building industry, for example, required a constant flow of men to work on houses for the vast numbers arriving in the town to work on the railways. Thanks to a lack of local planning strategies, and the entrepreneurship of the building trade, red-brick houses shot up all over the town. John Chandler, in *Swindon: History and Guide*, recounts the tale of 'Old Charlie', a tall, thin Yorkshireman who purchased Upper Eastcott Farm along with six stone cottages, and promptly set about the building of six further, brick-built dwellings and a shop. Naming his little terrace York Place, Old Charlie rented the properties out and, one imagines, spent the rest of his days as a prosperous landlord. Old Charlie's potential tenants would include working-class men who had arrived from as far afield as the North of England, as he had, or Wales. Mostly, the men would arrive singly or in small gangs, but occasionally they would turn up with their families too. All were looking for a way to earn a living, including many of the women, even before the war started to change gender roles in wider ways. Again, Swindon, with its Works, was well suited to these needs. Another industry

Modern Swindon was founded on the coming of the Great Western Railway, but, during the Great War, it was the Midland & South Western Junction Railway station in Old Town that was crucial for getting troops to their destinations in the South.

The official yearbook was a record of Swindon statistics, births, deaths, etc. It was all about to change.

BOROUGH OF SWINDON.

OFFICIAL
YEAR BOOK,
1914-1915.

that benefitted from the railways was 'the rag trade' – tailoring and clothes-making. Compton's clothes factory employed over 1,000 women in Swindon at the turn of the century, with much of their work being the production of GWR uniforms.

Even so, work was not always available, and with a steady influx of new jobseekers, competition could be tough. Without a job, people would struggle to find somewhere to live and often go hungry. For an agricultural worker on a failing farm, losing a job could also mean losing the family home. Heading into town was an obvious choice for many locals, as well as for those from further afield, but of course, then as now, employers needed the right kind of employees.

A Different Class of Soldier

In the late nineteenth century, Swindon writer Richard Jefferies observed that the GWR, emulating the class system that existed at the time, produced two kinds of employee: the 'working' engineers, many of them former agricultural workers or lads growing up in local villages; and the 'gentlemen' engineers, highly educated, well-qualified men, often coming to Swindon from elsewhere. This model was carried through to the huge new armies that were created to fight the war.

As elsewhere, Swindon in 1914 had a very visible class system, with the local lords of the manor being the Goddard family on their estate at the edge of Old Town. The Goddard's manor, known as The Lawns, was a grand affair with library, billiard room and gun room, and, outside, an arboretum, artificial lakes, and ornamental gardens for entertaining, holding garden parties and fetes. The house also had servants' quarters. On the other side of the town, the St John family owned the splendid Lydiard House. Set in a 260-acre deer park, the house is a Georgian Palladian mansion, redeveloped in the eighteenth century by then owner, John, 2nd Viscount Bolingbroke.

However, in 1914 the Industrial Revolution had created another layer of well-off folk, which included local business-men and the gentlemen engineers. A look at the top of the donations to the newly created Prince of Wales National Fund shows where the money was in Swindon as war broke out. At the very top is Thomas Arkell, co-owner of the local brewery, who donated a colossal £100. Next on the list, Thomas' co-owner and brother James gave £50, as did Lord of the Manor Fitzroy Pleydell Goddard, and Henry Kinneir, a solicitor and

At the time of the Great War, Swindon's GWR Works employed over 10,000 workers.

churchwarden. George Jackson Churchward, the now-legendary Chief Mechanical Engineer of the GWR, gave a healthy £30, and Henry Stanier, GWR Assistant Locomotive Works Manager donated £25.

The value of donations steadily decreased going down the list of Swindon's well-to-do, but the majority of people did not get onto the list at all. Another Swindon writer, Alfred Williams (*see* p.20), spent much of his time concerned with the other end of the social spectrum, such as the characters on the shop floor of the GWR where he worked before the war. In a later introduction to his *Life in a Railway Factory*, which was originally published in 1915, Leonard Clark sums up Williams' words:

> He describes, with consummate skill and admirable economy, the work of the shunters, watchmen, carriage finishers, painters, washers-down, cushion beaters, ash wheelers, road-waggon builders, smiths, fitters, boiler makers and moulders, to name but a few of the trades mentioned — many of them humble workmen but all necessary in the great enterprise of keeping the railways running. He introduces his readers to several of his mates — Herbert, the bricklayer's labourer, Baltimore, the drop stamper, Tubby, the best furnaceman in the works, Sambo and Strawberry, Budget and Charlie, the moulder — all characters in their own right, often amusing, sometimes tragic, and all seen in the atmosphere of noise, turmoil, coming and going, ceaseless travail. And as if to relieve all this, Williams notes the hares and rabbits that used to trespass into the factory yard, the profusion of wild flowers on the waste land, the rooks and sparrows, and, far away on the skyline, the blue of Liddington Hill with its hedges and chalk pits.

SWINDON'S WAR POET

In 1913, Alfred Williams was working in the GWR Works, living in poverty and suffering from various ailments, including acute dyspepsia. Over the years, Williams' friends and supporters tried to arrange for financial support, with the interest of three different prime ministers. However, Williams did not want charity, and despite being told he might only live another six months, continued working until just after the start of the war in September 1914, scrawling 'VICI' (I conquered) in chalk above his furnace when he finally left.

Williams' response to the war started with an anti-war (and anti-German) poem being published in the Swindon Advertiser on 24 August. He continued with his literary works, embarking on a collection of local folk songs and, in 1915, publishing his definitive book, Life in a Railway Factory. At the end of the year he had his War Sonnets and Songs published, though he later described them as 'little war scribbles' and 'of no value'. In September 1916, to his surprise and delight, the 39 year old was passed fit for war duty, on home duty with the Royal Field Artillery. But early in 1917 the unit moved to County Cork in Ireland, then across to Edinburgh, Scotland, then south again to the Royal Garrison Artillery in Winchester. In late 1917, Gunner Williams was posted to India, and spent seven weeks travelling on the Balmoral Castle with terrible conditions, food shortages and submarine attacks. In November, after stops in South Africa, Williams finally arrived in Bombay, where the journey carried on by train for another 1,600 miles to Roorkee – 'a place of noise and evil smells'.

In March 1918, Williams' battery moved to the unbearable heat of Cawnpore where Williams suffered, like many others, from diarrhoea, dysentery and fever. Despite the hardship and illnesses, Williams eventually fell in love with the country, writing: 'The Himalayas are divine … What material I shall have for books – if I live … I would not have missed India for five years of life.'

TO OUR ALLIES THE BELGIANS

(Julius Cæsar fought many fierce battles with the ancient
Belgians, and, notably, one on the banks of the river
Axona, now the Aisne. He described the Belgians as
the bravest of all the peoples of Western Europe.)

FORTISSIMI—" THE BRAVEST "—Cæsar said,
    Viewing their deeds of old ; and well he knew
    Their valour, though in numbers rare and few,
What time his hosts, to bloody battle led,
Stemmed the fierce charge, and heaped the fields with dead,
    Where that same Aisne her silent passage drew ;
    Still were they virtuous, fearless, bold and true,
And shunned not War's extremest paths to tread.
Glory to Belgium ! Twice ten hundred years
    Have dimmed not all the brightness of her name,
    Nor marred the tribute, Cæsar, which thou gavest ;
For, from her sacrifice of blood and tears,
    She stands emblazoned with triumphant fame,
    And still we write *FORTISSIMI*—" THE BRAVEST."

(22)

CHARGE OF THE 9th LANCERS

" In the wood upon our right
    Are the fierce insulting guns
Belching out their blackest spite
    Hot as hell on Freedom's sons ;
They are many, ye are few,
    But your hearts are noble all ;
Forward ! cleave a passage through,
    Firm against the iron wall !

" Where your faithful comrades lie,
    In the trenches fighting well,
Showers of murderous bullets fly,
    Searching shot and screaming shell ;
Ye can still them, and ye must.
    Up ! Away ! Be staunch and true.
In your strength is England's trust.
    Charge the Prussian battle crew ! "

Loudly as the summons rang
    Calling for a dauntless deed,
Every war-stained hero sprang
    High upon his prancing steed ;
Sprang, and naught in answer spake,
    Loosed his rein and bared his lance :
" Forward now, for England's sake !
    Furious on the foe advance ! "

(23)

Two of Williams' poems in his collection War Sonnets and Songs.

Alfred Williams (right) with comrades in the Royal Field Artillery in India.

Williams did not only make warm comments about fellow workers, and astute observations; his book also illustrates some of the considerably less comfortable aspects of life for those men who found themselves in the 'worker' class in 1914. Much to the horror of the GWR management, Williams describes the Works as a place of 'misery, cruelty, lack of initiative, waste, thieving and moral degradation behind the scenes …'

As war dawned, the romantic notion of 'the great age of steam' hid this tougher reality, and the same was true elsewhere in Swindon, and across the country. In Stratton St Margaret, the Swindon and Highworth Poor Law Union ran a 'busy' workhouse, a place described as every working-class person's nightmare. It was a place where anyone could end up through a stroke of bad luck, such as illness, an itinerant lifestyle, inade-quate provision for old age, lack of work, or simply an accidental twist of fate. Alfred Williams described the Swindon workhouse residents as tragic characters:

> Many have gone there to end their days, to die out of sight of all that is kind and charitable, doubting of life, doubting of love, of truth, fidelity, and friendship, doubting sometimes even of Providence itself – alone, forgotten, deserted for ever, forlorn and solitary.

Tough Times

For the majority, the workhouse was but a relatively distant threat, but life could still be tough. In October 1914, the *North Wilts Herald* cited an extract from David Hume's eighteenth-century *Treatise of Human Nature*, declaring, 'A man wants food, lodging, and clothing; a wife, children and friends; a daily occupation, by which, with either head or hand, he produces something more than he consumes, or otherwise does his share of the world's work.' But in 1914, these things were not always assured, par-ticularly because, perhaps above everything on Hume's list, what everyone wanted was good health.

When war broke out there was no social welfare infrastructure as we think of it today. Public sanitation and overall 'health and safety' was not of the same modern standards that we enjoy, and there was no health service for the general populace. However, despite Alfred Williams' condemnations, the GWR were one of the more progressive employers when it came to the welfare of their workers. If you were lucky enough to have a job in the Works you had considerable advantage over your neighbours, with the GWR's Medical Fund Society providing for doctor, dental and surgery services, public baths and the town's first hospital. Nonetheless, during 1916, even this social aid suffered. With so many men going off to fight in the services, huge gaps were left in the Works pool of skilled labour, and many of the men stopped paying their subscriptions to the Medical Fund Society. Families not only lost their breadwinners but also faced the possibility of losing access to medical help. During that year, the Society started running up debts at the bank, and staff salaries all but dried up. The impact of this 'trying state of affairs' led to the formation of a new dedicated committee and a levy which ultimately kept the Society going. The 1916 end-of-year report suggested that 'State Medical Service will undoubtedly be an ideal for the future, but our present Society could be a model miniature State organisation'. In fact, such was the ultimate success of the Swindon Medical Fund Society, that it became one of the models on which Health Secretary Aneurin Bevan based the National Health Service in 1948. With the extent of industry brought to the town by the GWR, and the positive attitude towards health that the company worked towards, it is no surprise that Swindon's motto is '*Salubritas et Industria*' – Health and Industry.

WAR.

ENGLAND AND GERMANY IN CONFLICT.

War announced on page 3 of the North Wilts Herald on 5 August 1914.

Inevitably, as the war got under way, it was assumed that further hardship would not be far behind, especially as winter conditions settled in. Nationally, people imagined that families would be plunged into poverty as men left their jobs to join up, and that the war would have a negative effect on business and industry, causing increased unemployment. However, it was also imagined that the hardships would be bearable since the war would 'All be over by Christmas'.

Melting Pot

Whether you were worker or gentleman, lord or pauper, young or old and male or female, the war was not over by Christmas, and was about to change everything. At the 'top' end of the class spectrum, Lord Suffolk became a major in the Swindon-based 3rd Wessex Brigade of the Royal Field Artillery; Thomas Arkell, top contributor to the Prince of Wales fund in the list outlined earlier, put the brewery aside and joined the Wiltshire Regiment, becoming a captain in the 4th Battalion and eventually serving in India, Mesopotamia and the Middle East. From Lydiard, two of the St John family joined up: Henry Mildmay St John enlisted as a lieutenant in the 11th Battalion Gloucestershire Regiment, was promoted to captain in January 1915 and sent home later that year after being shot through both thighs while on active service in the Dardanelles. His brother, Vernon Henry St John, 6th Viscount Bolingbroke, signed up as a private in the 3rd Devonshire Regiment, the only peer of the realm to do so. He stands as evidence of the complete lack of respect for class that the war had, returning from France shell-shocked before being discharged from the army. The St John estate, Lydiard, also provided men from the other end of the spectrum, with estate workers fighting alongside their masters. Arthur William Lockey, born in Lydiard Millicent, was one of twelve children and served with the 5th Wiltshire Battalion in Mesopotamia where, on 25 January 1917, he was killed in action at Kut, aged only 19. Another of his comrades on the estate, William Earnest Aldridge, was one of eight children. Aldridge, also 19, died of his wounds on 23 October 1918, after action on the Western Front with the Royal Garrison Artillery 281st Siege Battery.

Vernon Henry St John, 6th Viscount Bolingbroke, of Lydiard was the only peer of the realm to enlist as a private.

One local man, Owen Rutter, served as a lieutenant with the 7th Wiltshire battalion, and went on to describe his experiences in a parody of Longfellow's *The Song of Hiawatha*, which Rutter called *Tiadatha* (*Tired Arthur*). It is the story of a privileged young man who matures through his war experiences. In the opening verse, Tiadatha describes how life was for men like him before they joined up:

You could see him any morning
In July of 1914,
Strolling slowly down St James's
From his comfy flat in Duke Street.
Little recked he of in those days,
Save of socks and ties and hair-wash,
Girls and motor-cars and suppers ;
Little suppers at the Carlton,
Little teas at Rumpelmeyer's,
Little week-ends down at Skindle's ;
Troc and Cri and Murray's knew him,
And the Piccadilly grill-room,
And he used to dance at Ciro's
With the fairies from the chorus,
There were many Tired Arthurs
In July of 1914.
Then came war, and Tiadatha
Read his papers every morning,
Read the posters on the hoardings,
Read 'Your King and Country want you.'
'I must go,' said Tiadatha,
Toying with his devilled kidneys,
'Do my bit and join the Army.'

Purton boy Frank Sutton joined up aged 16 years and 4 months. He saw action in France and Mesopotamia and died of his wounds aged 18 on 30 March 1917.

The story of the 'workers', whether they were already in the reserves, volunteered at the start of the war, or later conscripted, is told throughout this book. The great irony for many of the poorer men who fought was that joining the army actually improved their health, through the regime of exercise and an improved diet. However, it is also true that many men who joined from Swindon, particularly those from the Works, were of a stronger, fitter physique than the average for the time. Unfortunately, none of this meant much in the trenches of Flanders, and no one was immune from the call. Even Alfred Williams, who wrote so passionately about his fellow workers, eventually joined up and served his country.

For women, the war would also alter everyday life. In 1900, only about 7.2 per cent of women in Swindon were in employment, but the overwhelming needs of the war were about to alter those figures forever. A chapter is devoted to women's roles later on, but what became clear to many from the outset of the war was the lunacy of jailing women for having demanded the right to vote. In the years leading up to 1914, the Swindon Suffragettes

Soldiers of 'H' Company, Wiltshire Regiment, relaxing at camp before being sent off to action.

R.J. and E.J. Walter and their younger sister Mabel getting into the spirit of things with her brother's uniform.

had created a strong and devoted group, with one woman standing out in particular. Swindon teacher, Edith New, after hearing Emmeline Pankhurst speaking in Trafalgar Square in 1907, joined the Women's Social and Political Union, and became one of the very first women to chain herself to railings, in Downing Street, for the cause. As a consequence of her actions, Edith spent several periods in prison, and she was not alone. In September 1914, the local press announced: 'Suffragettes & Strikers to be Released.' The article explained how the Home Secretary, in the House of Commons, had advised the king 'to remit the remainder of the sentences on all persons now undergoing terms of imprisonment for crimes connected with the Suffrage agitation'. Along with striking agricultural workers, any women imprisoned for crimes associated with suffrage were released with 'His Majesty confident the prisoners would respond to the feelings of their countrymen and women in this time of emergency, and could be trusted not to stain the causes they had at heart by any further crime and disorder'.

2

PREPARATIONS AT HOME

The sound of the GWR hooter was normally used to indicate the start or finish of shifts at the Works, but on 4 August 1914, its ten blasts formed the prearranged call to arms for local men in the army reserves and territorial units. Instantly the streets filled with men making their way to their respective centres: either the GWR Park in New Town, or the Drill Hall in Old Town, which already had four men on guard, with rifles and fixed bayonets. The numbers of men who already belonged to the various local units was substantial, with representation from every walk of life and just about every local company or organisation; for example, Swindon Post Office alone provided ten men. And, of course, everyone else came out to watch and cheer the soldiers on. War had been anticipated for some time; now it was here, and the town was alive with the excitement.

The steam hooters which blasted out the announcement of war above the GWR Works.

At 6.30 a.m. the following day, the Swindon Royal Army Medical Corps paraded in front of New Town Drill Hall and, by 9 a.m., an advanced guard of the Swindon Company of the Wilts (Fortress) Royal Engineers was already leaving Swindon from the GWR station. Later in the day, on the other side of town at the Midlands & South Western Junction (M&SWJ) station, the men, guns and equipment of the Wilts Battery and Ammunition Column of the 3rd Wessex Brigade Royal Field Artillery arrived, having been made ready during the day. They were joined by members of the council, Chief Officials

Swindon's Royal Field Artillery men, on Victoria Road, were mobilised on the day war was announced.

from the Corporation, the Countess of Suffolk, Lady Suffolk (whose husband, the earl, was a major in the unit), and the young Lord Andover and his two brothers, as well as a huge crowd of local people. The Mayor of Swindon, Alderman C. Hill, made a rousing speech to the eighty officers and men: 'You are leaving home and friends at the call of duty, and you can depend upon us to see that those homes and friends, where necessary, are cared for in your absence. We will see that they do not want. Our good wishes go with you, believing that you will, as worthy sons, uphold the best traditions of our fore-fathers … Be of good cheer. Good bye, Good luck, and God bless you all!' According to Bavin, the send-off was met with a 'great volume of cheers from the crowd', as the troops boarded a train bound for Portsmouth.

Although it is hard for us to imagine now, with our hindsight of what the war was to become, the overwhelming feelings at the start of the war was 'excitement and wild enthusiasm', with the shouting and cheering of the crowds going on all day, singing patriotic songs such as 'Rule Britannia' at the top of their voices. Even so, amid the exuberance, it was apparent that many wives, mothers, sisters and sweethearts were struggling 'to restrain their feelings at parting from their loved ones'. And it was not only the women who were affected, as the *North Wilts Herald* reported:

In some cases there were pathetic farewell scenes, when young fellows, with no knowledge as to where they were to be drafted, were compelled to tear themselves away from relatives and friends, and with as much cheerfulness as they could command place themselves in readiness to serve their country.

The sense of euphoria was masking other less positive feelings too. Local woman, Hilda Fisher, recalls being in the crowd, aged 14, when her mother asked a man what all the fuss was about: 'He said, "Haven't you heard love, war's been declared?" I thought it was dreadful, all I could do was say, "Let's go home mother, please can we go home?"'

Nonetheless, the 'gunners' themselves were in good spirits, all keen to prove their loyalty to King and Country. Just a week earlier, they had returned from their annual training at Larkhill Camp on Salisbury Plain, where they excelled themselves. Not only did they win a cup, they were also told by Brigadier General Fanshawe that their drill 'was the best he had ever witnessed in Territorial Troops'. As their train set off towards Portsmouth, the men, under the command of Colonel Bedford Pim and Major the Earl of Suffolk, had no idea that ultimately they would be serving their time in India, reaching there in 1915.

Local dignitaries seeing off the first Swindon troops at Old Town railway station.

The GWR hooter gave another ten blasts on Thursday 6th, this time to summon the local squadron ('D' Squadron) of the Royal Wiltshire Yeomanry. Again, a large crowd turned up to see them off from the M&SWJ station. Though, on this occasion, the trip was not as dramatic as many, with the men simply spending the night on guard duty on the railways, before returning again the following day. Though, like most soldiers, the Yeomanry did go on later to see more serious action in France.

A Quieter Start

Swindonian Herbert Hillier Dunn joined the marines around 1908, aged 17 (pictured). He was in Belgium before Britain officially joined the war.

Not everyone was to receive such a rapturous send-off however. The naval reserves and Royal Marines, to which a number of Swindon men belonged, had already been called up on Sunday, 2 August. Over the days and weeks that followed the outbreak of war, many more men left Swindon, often with no more pomp or ceremony than the goodbyes and tears of family and friends. These included members of the army reserve – men who had signed up previously but not served their full twelve years. On this basis, a man who had served three years would be expected to remain with the reserves for another nine years. On top of this, there was the National Reserve which was in some ways more like the Territorial Army that we know today, where civilians (as well as ex-soldiers) could join up. At that time, many of the members were in older age brackets, up to the 42 years of age upper limit for service. In 1914, Swindon had 1,300 such men, organised into twelve companies, with many of them joining the 4th Wiltshire Battalion for home defence duties. For example, men of the Swindon No. 1 Company volunteered to fulfil duties relating to the guarding of tunnels, bridges and other important places along the railway lines, perhaps unsurprisingly given that many of them would have worked in the GWR Works.

Swindon men of 'D' Squadron, Royal Wiltshire Yeomanry.

Beyond the reserve forces that already existed, recruitment for the main army had of course started across the country. On 11 August, the Mayor of Swindon announced the creation of a Swindon Volunteer (Temporary) Force, aimed at recruiting men between 17 and 30. The initial plan was that the unit would be part of the Territorial Force, with drill practice on four evenings and Saturdays, under the command of Major F.P. Goddard and Sergeants Archer, Morse, Trimmer and Woolford. By September, approximately 200 men had joined up, with sixty of them quickly moving on to 'Kitchener's Army', and 100 of them joining local units, such as the Yeomanry and the Royal Field Artillery.

The First Casualties of War

Even while the 'celebrations' were still underway, the reality of war started to filter through from the front, as letters from serving Swindon men appeared in the local press. These included reports from those fighting at sea, and from soldiers in France. At the 'Great Retreat' on 23 August, Swindon men were among those pushed back from Mons to the River Marne by the Imperial German Armies. Swindonians were also present at the first

Swindonian army reservist, Lance Corporal W.J. Nurden, was killed crossing the railway line. He was buried with full military honours in December 1914, in Swindon.

battles of Aisne and of Marne, both in September, and some were among the small numbers of British troops aiding the Belgians at the Siege of Antwerp in the first two months of the war.

The earliest report of a Swindon man being killed in action came early in September. William George Sheldon, who worked as an artificer in the engine rooms of HMS *Pathfinder*, was among those killed when the ship was devastated by a mine in the North Sea on 5 September. *Pathfinder*'s short role in the war made news of another, equally tragic, sort, in that she was the first ship to be destroyed by a self-propelled torpedo fired from a submarine (the German U-21). Around the same time, news came in about the death of Captain Gerald Ponsonby, the son of a previous vicar of St Mark's church in Swindon. Ponsonby died from wounds received in action while serving with the 2nd Battalion Royal Inniskilling Fusiliers.

It was not only the battlefield where tragedies occurred. Another of Swindon's early military casualties was a member of the army reserves, Lance Corporal W.J. Nurden, who was killed crossing the railway line at Newton Toney, near Salisbury, on his way to relieve another guard who had fallen sick. He was buried with full military honours in December 1914, in Swindon.

Swindon's first 'casualty' of the war was a Royal Naval reservist by the name of Shail, of Manchester Road. While packing for departure, Shail had a problem with a sticking drawer, and pulled it so hard that the whole cupboard fell on top of him, breaking his leg and injuring his back.

A Friendly Invasion

Preparations for war had been taking place for many years in military and political circles, and in 1914, the Committee for Imperial Defence set into motion plans laid down in what was known as the 'War Book'. The book detailed the actions of all major bodies, including railways and post offices, as well as providing plans for the gathering of regular military forces and the utilisation of reservists, as well as timetables for recruiting new volunteers. For Swindon, the effect of this mobilisation had a colossal impact in terms of sheer scale, with enormous numbers of men arriving in the town almost from the outset. The local press described Swindon, probably without exaggeration, as 'The principle centre for the embodiment of men for service either at home or abroad'. Many of the thousands of men who arrived were simply passing through, via the two stations, but inevitably many also needed to be billeted and provided for, for varying lengths of time.

The mayor issued an appeal 'To ask all householders on whom soldiers may be billeted to do the best they can for the men and to give them a kindly welcome. It will mean some inconvenience, but I am sure we are all willing to put up with this in this great national emergency.' As a consequence, locals opened up their homes, taking in as many as they could physically fit and sometimes with five or six soldiers taking up every inch of floor space. For those who were well off, or had larger premises, billeting a few soldiers was not an issue, and even when space was tight the householders 'cheerfully complied with the wishes of the authorities'. However, for some, putting up soldiers was more than just an inconvenience. The Gee family, who took in three soldiers, also had a baby and other children to look after. As a consequence, 13-year-old Clarice Gee was often kept at home to help her mother, instead of going to school. This was considered unacceptable, with the magistrate's clerk stating that the child's education must come first, and levying a fine of 7s 6d on the family.

The job of guiding the men, all strangers to the town, fell to the Boy Scouts. The Scouts took over a room in the Town Hall as their headquarters and, under the leadership of Mr W. Arnold-Forster, worked tirelessly day and night to help the visitors. At the same time, halls and schools were requisitioned; for example, the Higher Elementary School, Westcott School, Ferndale Road School and Clarence Street School were all taken over as temporary barracks, or mess rooms, leaving some of the teachers taking up needle and thread to repair damaged uniforms instead of educating local children. Inevitably, more permanent solutions were required (and they would soon come), but the war could not wait for new buildings to be erected as the stream of men responding to Kitchener's call to arms continued to pour into the town.

The local Scouts, in this case the Tyler brothers from 2nd Swindon Scouts, were responsible for guiding troops around the town.

On 21 August 1914, Army Order No. 324 authorised the formation of six new divisions, to create Kitchener's new army, K1. The volunteers joining these divisions quickly began assembling south of Swindon, on Salisbury Plain, with 40th Brigade massing at Cirencester and Chiseldon in September. In a matter of weeks, four battalions, some 5,000 men, were camped out in the muddy fields of Draycot Foliat and Chiseldon on the edge of Swindon: the men made up the 8th Battalion Cheshire Regiment, 8th Battalion Royal Welsh Fusiliers, 8th Battalion Welsh Regiment, and 4th Battalion South Wales Borderers. It became an everyday occurrence for locals to see columns of men marching across the town, often arriving at the New Town GWR railway station and transferring to the M&SWJ station in Old Town, either on their way to Chiseldon, or heading on to camps elsewhere. It is odd to think that, besides the train and walking, the most common forms of transport in 1914 were still horse-drawn vehicles, and that was as true for the military as it was for everyone else, with carts and wagons moving men and equipment along the muddy lanes throughout the makeshift campsite at Chiseldon.

It was not only British troops that passed through Swindon. These men are ANZACs, from Australia and New Zealand.

A Different Kind of Shortage

The men who came into Swindon were usually greeted with proud and patriotic cheers by the locals, admiring the 'gallantry' of early visitors from the Scottish Division for example. Some men, however, unfairly received a little less respect.

In late 1915, the town became a temporary home to the 'Bantams', men who failed to reach the required minimum height of 5ft 3in (1.6m) to serve. The idea behind these groups of men came from Alfred Bigland, MP for Birkenhead in 1914, who suggested that there were plenty of perfectly fit men available whose only 'issue' was their height. The army responded by permitting special battalions to be created, with a number of regiments eventually adopting the idea, including: Bigland's local regiment – the Cheshire Regiment; the Lancashire Fusiliers; the West Yorkshire Regiment; the Royal Scots; and the Highland Light Infantry.

While the Bantams were based in Swindon, they became a familiar sight around the town, especially on Saturday evenings. The men were popular with the locals, and even though Bavin describes 'the ludicrous sight' of a group of Bantams, his comments also suggest that it was the taller men who looked odd: 'a picket of Bantams strutting slowly in file whilst a thin sergeant of six feet in height ambled along the pavement vainly trying to find a step that would harmonise with that of his picket, and painfully conscious of his unseemly stature.'

New Life

When the men signed up for the forces, many of them doubtlessly thought they would be given a uniform and a gun and packed off to face 'the Hun', and were keen and eager to do so. But military life is not like that. First of all the men had to undergoing training, which for most would mean many months before seeing any action. Ronald Percival Clack, from Rodbourne, was a coppersmith at the GWR Works and had great hopes for his future. He saw 4 August 1914 as 'an event that upset all his plans'. After wrestling with his conscience and

Training included all things military, as well as physical fitness.

deciding the war was for a just cause, he and two colleagues, Walter Loveday and Jesse Hollick, volunteered for the Royal Field Artillery at the end of August.

Clack gives us an idea of what life was like for new men in the army, describing overcrowded barracks, congested training sessions and the complete chaos at meal times. In terms of his colleagues, he describes a 'motley collection of people' including university undergraduates, manual workers, men from respectable homes, and some he thought of as being 'scum of the Earth'. Before long, he and his comrades were moved on to the Shorncliff barracks, in Kent, but, again because of overcrowding, they ended up in bell tents – not a pleasant experience in the cold of autumn and winter. With some experience as a signaller in the Boy Scouts, Clack was selected for training in army signalling, and successfully passed his training in semaphore, Morse code and heliograph. But, because the artillery of 1914 was reliant on horses, Clack also had to complete training in horsemanship, executed under the leadership of the 'unfriendly' Captain Caddington: 'it would appear that one of his hobbies was to put fear into anyone, and I don't doubt whether anyone went through his school unscathed or without falling off.' Nonetheless, Clack succeeded and was sent off to have his inoculations ready for

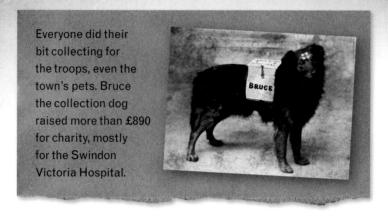

Everyone did their bit collecting for the troops, even the town's pets. Bruce the collection dog raised more than £890 for charity, mostly for the Swindon Victoria Hospital.

overseas service. Unfortunately, it turned out he was one of those for whom the medicines had a bad effect, and spent the next ten weeks recuperating in a convent, thinking his military career was over before it even began.

But it was not over. Clack was passed fit for service, and joined up with his battery in France on 5 May. As a signaller with the Royal Field Artillery (C Battery 62nd Brigade 12 Division), he saw action at Loos, Arras, Cambrai and St Quentin. On the Somme, 1–3 July 1916, he was awarded the Military Medal, and, on 13 September 1918, he was wounded by shell fire and gas simultaneously, suffering bad wounds to both legs and being temporarily blinded. Another Swindon man in the same battery as Clack, John Henry Huntley, also won the Military Medal, but died on 25 October 1916. Clack escaped that fate, but still underwent terrible suffering. After recovering from his wounds at a base hospital, he fell ill with pneumonia and was eventually sent back to England where he remained in hospital until March 1919. Clack went on to live a long life, eventually writing down his memories of the 'horrors of war' when he was 84.

The Mighty Landship

For Swindon-born William George Blake, whose company was drafted from the Royal Engineers, training was like nothing anyone had ever experienced before. He was one of the first men to drive one of the brand new tanks.

A need for armoured vehicles was acknowledged from the outset of the war. Curiously, it was the navy rather than the army which first began investigating ideas, with the Royal Naval Air Service (RNAS) deploying the earliest examples in France in the early days of the war, manned by Royal Marines and the Royal Naval Division. Swindon man Herbert Hillier Dunn was in the Royal Marines when they were sent out to France, even before the main British Expeditionary Force. However, the initial tactic of using armoured vehicles was short-lived. By October 1914, a level of battlefield stalemate was already established across France, with trenches rendering most vehicles redundant. Nonetheless, designers continued to work on ideas, but with an emphasis on creating something that could deal with the new conditions. As a consequence, a 'landship' committee was created in February 1915 by Winston Churchill, First Lord of the Admiralty, and soon the first tanks were rolling into France. Although early experiences were not too successful, the tanks improved. Field Marshall Haig ordered the building of 1,000 vehicles and, on 27 July 1917, a Tank Corps was officially formed with Blake being one of its first recruits.

Blake's memoirs tell how surprised he was when he and eleven comrades, all in new brown dungarees, first saw the colossal Mark 1 tanks which they were to learn to drive. Shaken and deafened by the huge 105hp engine, and overwhelmed by the fumes and heat, Blake had to get to grips with the controls amid shouts of 'Get her into neutral!' and 'No, not that one, the other!' He also describes how he looked through his cab flap and was 'astounded' to see somebody calmly wandering past him. Despite all the noise and bumping about, the tank was only going at 2¼ miles an hour.

Blake soon learned the tricks of the tank, and became adept at navigating it over trenches. He was particularly glad to be the driver, securely strapped into his seat, while his colleagues were thrown about in the rear. Eventually, Blake took the official driver's test, driving the tank around a specially designed course which ended with the 'Swallow Dive', up an incline, over a precipice and then an 'alarming plunge into a deep shell hole'. It was an ordeal with serious threat of failure and possible injury, which the drivers all dreaded. But Blake was equal to the task.

Following further training in maintenance, and firing the tank's 6-pounder guns, he went on a month's course to become a tank-driving instructor himself. After two weeks' leave, Blake was sent to a driving school in France, based at the Tank Corps' transit camp at Le Treport, where he spent several weeks teaching men to drive Mark IV tanks. Following this, Blake moved to a new driving school at Wailly-Sautrecourt, near the front line, where much-improved Mark V tanks were arriving at the rate of about sixty per week. Here, Blake met another trainer, Jack Few, who was also from Swindon, the son of a butcher on Faringdon Road.

The Realities of War

Of course, training did not stop when the men were on active service. The Wiltshires, in advance of an attack on Messines, were given eight days of training at nearby Esquerdes, where the men were drilled into learning seventeen points by heart. The top five points were:

1. Men must anticipate a counter attack
2. Men must not stop to attend to the wounded
3. If a nest of machine guns is encountered, or any strong point, it must be dealt with at once
4. Beware of people dressed as staff officers
5. There is no such word as 'retire'

The list gives some idea of the expectations on the men, especially points three and five. The fourth point is intriguing, and the second point really brings home the cruel reality of what the men would be facing when they finally entered the battlefields themselves.

3

WORK OF WAR

In retrospect, one of the curiosities of the early days of the war was the idea of 'life carrying on'. There are two sides to this idea: the optimistic aspiration that the war would not last long enough to really change anything, and the necessity to deal with everyday issues just as before. These views are exemplified by a scan of any newspaper from the first months of the war. As well as the columns devoted to conflict (and these were not as dominant as we might think), there was all the local news being treated with the same importance as it was before the war started. The pages still carried advertisements too, telling the world about the wonderful quality of local products, all at bargain prices. In fact, in 1915, the *Swindon Advertiser* carried an advert of its own, declaring: 'Advertising Pays at All Times. It is a great mistake for traders to restrict their advertising to prosperous times. The science of advertising is to produce trade. Not a Luxury but a Necessity should be your motto.' Business, like the rest of life, had to carry on.

Business as Usual

On Monday, 3 August 1914, the front page of the *Evening North Wilts Herald* was focused, as it always was, on news of 'Agriculture and Gardening Notes', giving seasonal advice on potatoes, greenhouse cultures, and weed extirpation. On Tuesday 4th, it was the same, with a small announcement on page 3 that

England was prepared now war had arrived. The front page news was the same again on Wednesday, but page 3 declared: 'WAR. ENGLAND AND GERMANY IN CONFLICT.' Of course the paper soon changed its approach, but its early editions are evidence of a determination to carry on regardless; that the war was not going to affect the 'important' things.

In the GWR Works, the plan was also 'business as usual'. But it was not going to be as straightforward as that. The company itself may have decided to continue running its normal services, but the war was to have great need for what the Works could do. Although the place was a railway factory, the fact that the men usually engaged in railway-related tasks did not mean that was the limit of their skills, nor the limits of the tools and machines they used. The site was first and foremost an engineering works, full of highly skilled engineers, mechanics, carpenters, etc. The War Office, or more specifically the Royal Ordnance Department, had good use for those skills. On the day war was declared, the National Railway Executive Committee (REC), which had been formed in 1912, produced an Order in Council that handed authority of the majority of the country's railways over to the government. The idea was that everything would be

A military water cart in front of the GWR Works, with all the components needed to produce one laid in front.

run exactly as before, but with priority going to national needs. For Swindon Works, this meant not only provision of rolling stock, locomotives, etc., but also special services for freight and troop movements, and the production of myriad other items, ranging from gun carriages and artillery shells, to horse-drawn water-carriers and personal webbing straps.

More than Trains

On top of normal production, the Works' main contribution was, despite the breadth of items produced, still in the production of vehicles, most of them for the railways. Two classes of locomotive were commissioned, both selected because of their power, sturdiness of build and dependability – the Dean Good 2301 class, and the slightly older style Armstrong Goods class, all painted in black. Exact records for what was built are sketchy, mainly because of the imperative of secrecy during the war, but the war record of the GWR estimates that some ninety-five

A carriage for an ambulance train being lowered onto the track.

In August 1914, as the first two ambulance trains were completed at the GWR Works, the townspeople flocked to see them, paying 6d each, with a stream of visitors forming a queue four deep continuously between 2 p.m. and 6 p.m.

locomotives were built specially, plus 105 tenders. These engines were sent all over the world; for example, three Armstrongs were sent to Serbia in August 1916, and eight more were ferried to Salonika in May 1917, only to be lost when their transport ship was sunk by the enemy in the English channel. Another eight engines, of the 388 class, were eventually sent in their place. The majority of locomotives, however, ended up in France, some sixty-two in all. The GWR also built locomotives to lend to other railways in England and abroad, and although most of the new machines eventually came back, some stayed where they were, ending their days working for foreign companies like the Ottoman Railway in Turkey.

To accompany the locomotives, the Works also produced hundreds of wagons and carriages. For example, 410 high-sided, open-horse wagons were built almost immediately, followed by 101 side-less open wagons, 171 paired sets of timber trucks, and 213 rail and timber vehicles specifically designed for transporting artillery guns, limbers, carts, etc. One particularly special commission involved the production of ambulance trains. By the end of the war, 238 carriages for these were constructed, including bedded wards,

Inside one of the specially commissioned ambulance carriages made in Swindon, with nurses at the ready.

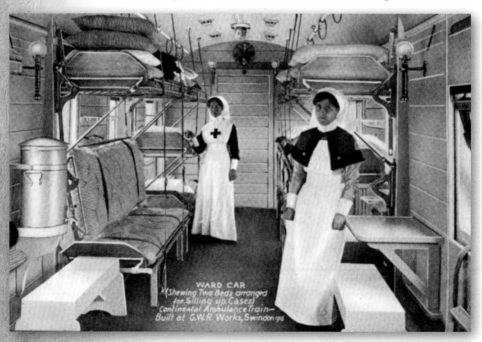

WARD CAR
(Shewing Two Beds arranged
for Sitting up Cases)
Continental Ambulance Train—
Built at G.W.R Works, Swindon

infectious case wards, staff carriages, kitchens, offices, messes, pharmacies, or stores. Most of the ambulance trains were sent to France, though some were held back on this side of the Channel to ferry injured and sick men from the ports, such as Southampton, to hospitals dotted around the country, including one at Chiseldon on the edge of Swindon (*see* 'Looking After the Wounded' in this chapter). A further 638 coaches were built to provide new services, primarily to get workers to and from munitions factories, many of which were sited outside towns and cities, for obvious reasons.

Besides the extra railway vehicles, the Works also produced 1,100 horse-drawn road wagons and fifty special water carts. By the end of the war the whole of the GWR had produced a staggering 216,350 vehicles, and a colossal number of these had come out of the Works at Swindon.

> In 1915, ten battalions of warriors on bicycles were created. The Army Cyclist Corp set up its headquarters at Chiseldon, to send men out as the first line of defence along England's coastlines. The cyclists' mobility, plus specialist fieldcraft, musketry and demolition skills were intended to deal with an invasion which, thankfully, never came.

Munitions

It was not only vehicles that the Works produced. Large areas of the Swindon Works were given over to the specialised production of munitions, with new manufacturing equipment being brought in or created, processes being squeezed into smaller areas, and a number of new spaces being created. Because of the erratic nature of the records, the following are given as examples of what was turned out of the Swindon shops:

- A complete factory-line was created in X Shop, dedicated to the production of 6in high-explosive shells. Over the two and a half years the production carried on, the shop used 265,652 tons of steel and made 2,500 shells per week – a total of 325,000
- For the navy, rotary davits (ship cranes) that were 3ft 6in in diameter and 14ft tall
- Production of 18-pounder field gun shells, including 1,863,000 copper driving bands, 103,127 graze fuses, and 484,566 other fuses

- 384,651 major components for other types of shells
- Large field carriages for forty massive, 6in-calibre naval guns, including heavy riveted plate made in the boiler shop. Carriages also involved the creation of cradles, trunnions, actuating gear, worm driven elevating quadrants, and all requiring a very high standard of engineering
- Manufacturing line for 6-pounder Nordenfelt anti-aircraft guns, plus 6-pounder Hotchkiss and Woolwich pattern guns
- Fabricated parts for 4.5in howitzers and 60-pounder guns, using highly complicated upset forgings – 338 gun carriages and carriage limbers, 1,078 ammunition wagons and limbers. A total of 224,769 separate components
- Carriages and limbers for a dozen colossal, 8in howitzers
- 50lb–70lb aircraft bombs
- 3,850 wooden posts for picketing horses, plus 38,000 pegs
- 2,950 stretchers

This list outlines some of the main things produced at the Works, but it is impossible to account for the countless smaller objects and parts created. For example, the skills of the carriage fitters, particularly in Trimming (No. 9) Shop, were also employed to make thousands upon thousands of pieces of leatherwork for things like mule pack saddlery, cases, carrying bags, and even straps for individual soldier equipment.

The GWR Works produced countless munitions, and manufactured weapons such as these 6in 'naval' guns.

Hard Times; Soft Furnishings

Some companies embraced the limits imposed by war. An advert from Liptons showed a smiling girl offering the delights of 'Margarine Overweight' made with nuts and cream, and described as 'Nutritious as butter and costs half the price!' There were some oddities too. Another advertisement at the time, from the curiously named RA-BA-SA, offered the chance for you to have your very own 'Radio-Active Bath at Home'. There was also an element of denial, demonstrating an uncertainty about the permanence of the war, on both sides of the Channel. On 11 November, the *Swindon Advertiser* carried an advert for 'Special Courses at the Dresden Royal Conservatoire for Music and Drama', with the courses taking place in Germany the following April and September. Almost certainly a waste of a marketing budget.

Inevitably, competition did not get any easier with the war, and special offers were commonplace. Essential items, such as coal and coke, were advertised by long-standing local company, Toomer's, where you could 'Solicit Orders at Lowest Market Prices'. Even large luxury items were still being advertised, though prices were being cut here too, perhaps unsurprisingly. Two local music firms, Duck, Son & Pinker and C. Milsom & Son, competed with each other in promoting 'Great Sales' and 'Popular Prices' for their large selections of pianos. Other adverts of the time, even early in autumn 1914, appeared to have hard-pressed

troops in mind, or at least customers who might buy goods for improving trench life for relatives. Bays, in Old Town, advertised its stoves as being 'A Real Boon in Wet and Cold Weather', and, when suffering 'Mental or Physical Fatigue', there was always Allenbury's Diet, for recovering the system's 'tone and vigour'.

One local firm, Gilberts, (which is still going today on Wood Street in Swindon) consistently advertised its services and wares in the local papers, and the content of the ads shows an interesting development in the company's sales approach. Just before the war, Gilbert's advertising used a hand-drawn/lettered image promoting the company's services in house furnishings, carpets, curtains etc., and proudly boasted its awards for excellence in Design Workmanship & Materials. As the war got under way, the straplines changed, replacing the arts and crafts feel with the optimistic quote: 'In time of War prepare for Peace, by purchasing Gilbert's furniture and carpets', for 'A Beautiful Home'. But the business was about to take a new turn.

The Military Customer

It was clear early on, as more and more men became involved, that new training camps and barracks would be required to service the military machine. At Swindon, land near Draycot Foliat and Chiseldon was already home to thousands of tented men. The site was purchased by the War Office and work began to build a more permanent facility. Given the name of Chiseldon Camp, it was soon joined up to the M&SWJ railway by the laying of a new branch running from near the station at Chiseldon, while

Adverts from Gilberts furniture supplier, showing how their marketing changed during the war.

barracks were built on the site itself. The buildings, according to the *North Wilts Herald*, were built of wood with corrugated iron roofs and asbestos linings, and cost the considerable sum of between £15,000–£16,000. In total, seventy-two buildings were constructed, each of them 50ft long and 20ft wide, designed to accommodate thirty men with all their kit, as well as a separate room for the NCO and, of course, toilets and a washhouse. Even before these were completed, on 12 October another order was placed with local company, H & C Spackman, for a further seventy-two buildings – such was the rate at which men were arriving.

But it was the inside of the barracks that created an opportunity for Gilberts, with the firm supplying fixtures and fittings such as beds and kit lockers. Their adverts changed again, promoting the firm as 'Camp Furnishers, Swindon and Chiseldon Camp', and making a point of being a War Office Contractor. Such was the success of the firm that they actually received a telegram from Kitchener in gratitude for the services they provided:

I wish to impress upon those employed by you the importance of the government work upon which they are engaged. I fully appreciate the efforts the employees are making, and the quality of the work turned out. I trust that everything will be done to assist the military authority by pushing on as rapidly as possible. I should also like all engaged by you to know that it is fully recognised that they, in carrying out the work of helping to supply accommodation for the troops, are doing their duty for their King and country equally with those who have joined the army for active service in the field.

A TANK
CALLED JULIAN

One of the ways funds were raised for the war was through National War Bonds. In March 1918, the Chancellor of the Exchequer, Bonar Law, sent a message to the Mayor of Swindon: 'I know that I can depend upon your doing your utmost. Every War Bond bought this week will show Germany to what extent we are in earnest.' In response the mayor launched a campaign, reminding people that that the town was in competition with other places, and appealing to the 'loyalty and patriotism of the inhabitants'. Despite the fact that the local banks and post offices had already issued some £150,000 worth of bonds that year, the town raised £84,621 in the seven days leading up to 'Campaign Week', and another £85,073 during the week itself.

A second campaign was launched in May 1918, but this time the focus of effort revolved around HM Tank, No. 113, named *Julian*, and the campaign was renamed 'Tank Week'. Following a 'leaflet-drop' from an aeroplane, *Julian* parked in the market square on the Monday, which was Farmers' Day, with a band of pipers from the London Scottish regiment and speeches from the mayor, the President of the Farmers' Union, and the vicar. In the evening, surrounded by huge crowds, the tank made its way down to the town hall, accompanied by the band of the Worcester Regiment. A huge barrier of sand-bags and barbed wire was created for the tank to tackle, which it did, slowly and until it was almost vertical, before spending the rest of the week outside the town hall.

Children sent to buy War Savings Certificates were able to get them stamped inside the tank. With the mayor purchasing the first £50 certificate, the town raised £115,000, including £20,000 from the GWR and £5,000 from the Swindon Corporation. By the end of the war, these and other such campaigns in Swindon raised over £1 million.

HM Tank,
No. 113 Julian in
Regent's Circus in
May 1918.

DROPPED FROM A BRITISH AEROPLANE.

"Go to the Tank and buy Bonds and Certificates, for EVERY PENNY lent to your country shortens the War, and brings an Honourable PEACE nearer."

LET SWINDON LEAD!

Morris Bros., "Advertiser" Office, Swindon.

Leaflet dropped
from an aeroplane
over Swindon,
encouraging
people to buy
bonds from
Julian the tank.

Looking after the Wounded

Another important aspect of wartime work back home was, inevitably, that of hospital provision for men wounded in action. In Swindon, before such hospital cover was provided, the vicar of the town offered his vicarage to the Red Cross. At the same time, training of medics at all levels of competence began, not only in Swindon, but in the outlying towns as well; for example, the first certificates for first-aid trainees in Wootton Bassett were awarded in October 1914. The students were taught by Dr Bogle, and examined by Dr F. Lewarne from Cricklade. One of the early recipients of a certificate was Julia Morgan, born in Switzerland and married to Revd David Morgan who was the pastor of the Congregational church in Wootton Bassett. Julia founded the Wootton Bassett Red Cross, which held its early meetings in Priory Cottage, built in 1266 as the Hospital of St John.

However, with men pouring into the area by the thousands, this was clearly insufficient. On 8 October, the Red Cross took over the public bathhouse on Milton Road, kitting it out as a temporary hospital. The GWR stepped in too, providing blankets, pillows and other items, as well as an endless supply of springs for the making of new mattresses. The hospital did well, and received considerable public support, especially at Christmas with a glut of donations of plum puddings, fruit and, ironically from today's

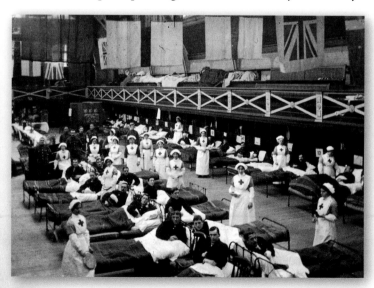

Hospital created in the swimming baths on Milton Road to fulfil emergency needs.

perspective, cigarettes! By the end of February 1915, the hospital had admitted 815 military patients and dealt with some 2,000 out-patients. Unfortunately, the hospital soon proved to be too small, with nearly 150 patients on some nights. Moreover, as the summer started to warm up, the glass roof, designed to keep bathers warm, made the place unbearably hot for the sick. However, provision for the sick had already been planned for the camp at Chiseldon and, in June 1915, a hospital opened there, making it possible to close the Milton Road site in July. The new hospital created yet another sales opportunity for Gilbert's. Before long, their adverts switched to this new focus entirely, adding a large medical cross and listing the goods they sold, with special offers for hospital beds, especially if purchased with all the accessories: bolsters, pillows, pillow cases, blankets and quilts. The adverts also carried a list of all the other local hospitals that Gilbert's supplied: Swindon Red Cross Hospital, Swindon Victoria Hospital, Swindon Isolation Hospital and Swindon and Highworth Infirmary.

At first the new hospital at Chiseldon, under the command of Colonel A.R. Hall, of the Royal Army Medical Corps (RAMC), had six wards each with twenty-four beds, and a staff of some forty nurses. Even after the capacity was practically doubled, an array of temporary wards in tents was usually pitched nearby too, giving a total of more than 500 beds. It makes sense that the RAMC would be involved at the new hospital but, ironically, it was not Swindon troops who were assigned to the task, even though the town did have its own unit of Wiltshire RAMC (Territorials Forces). Commanded by Major Surgeon Rodway Swinhoe, who was chief medical officer at the GWR Works, the Swindon unit comprised of 114 men at the outset of the war. Their name soon changed to 1/1 South Western Mounted Brigade Field Ambulance, and two other units were also created: 2/1 and 3/1. All three units, eventu-ally totalling some 320 men from Swindon, spent the early years of the war in places such as Winchester, Brighton, Eastbourne, Grundisburgh and Blackpool, with much of their time occupied by the 'monotony' of lectures on field ambulance work, nursing, diseases and sanitation. On occasion, the dull routine caused the men to look for any sort of change. At harvest time in 1916, some of those with agricultural experience were 'allowed' to help out on farms in Gloucestershire.

In 1914, newspaper adverts show F.M. Morse, a watchmaker and jeweller, offering 'Acceptable Presents for Christmas', and Chudleigh's were tempting customers with fur sets, handkerchiefs in boxes, gloves, blouses, umbrellas, etc., all at the 'lowest prices'.

However, as increasing numbers of casualties returned from France, the men of the RAMC found themselves being called on for work at British hospitals, such as the vast hospital services in Ipswich. In January 1917, an order from Brigadier General the Earl of Shaftesbury led to many men being split up from their units and sent out to wherever they were needed. As the general told them, 'Every "A1" man is urgently required in the field.' From then on, RAMC men found themselves being posted to field ambulance units in France, Mesopotamia, Russia, India, Macedonia and Saloniki. These men attended to the wounded (sometimes the enemy as well as their own comrades) in terrible conditions, risking their lives and sometimes making the ultimate sacrifice themselves; Swindon lost Privates Bangs, Beales, Blackwell, Bown, Crocker, Gleed, Greer, Lambert, Manning, Morris, Roxon, Schofield, and Vokins.

Throughout the war, a steady stream of wounded men flowed from the front lines to the hospital at Chiseldon, particularly after major battles. The military's (and the hospital's) efficient

A group of Royal Army Medical Corps men pose informally with a few family members in 1914.

systems were first put fully to the test after the Battle of Loos in autumn 1915, a battle in which the Wiltshire Regiment and Swindon men were involved. They would have had other things on their mind, but on the same day as they were fighting at Loos, the local newspaper reported that Stonehenge, the well-known landmark of their home county, was down as Lot 15 for sale at the Salisbury auction.

Bad Boys

It was not only shrapnel or bullet wounds that were treated at Chiseldon. One of the well-known but less talked about issues of war is the spread of venereal disease (VD), sexually transmitted diseases contracted by men away from home, taking solace wherever they could find it. During the course of the war nearly 500,000 men of the Allied Forces contracted some form of VD or other. This was a serious problem for the army, which could ill afford to have men off sick through 'careless passions'. As a consequence, and because civilian hospitals did not at that time have facilities for treating such patients, a new specialist area was built at the hospital at Chiseldon, with over 1,000 beds and nicknamed the 'Bad Boys' Hospital'. Unsurprisingly, the military authorities did not advertise the purpose of the unit too much, though it did not take long for people to figure it out for themselves. As David Bailey says, in his treatise on the camp:

Winifred Smith with her staff at the Navy, Army and Air Force Institutes at Chiseldon Camp. Mary's brother George was killed in action in Salonika in 1917.

> No matter what the authorities do, soldiers and girls will always get together. The 6.45 pm workmen's train from Swindon Old Town to Chiseldon was known to both the troops and the local inhabitants as the 'Meat Train' because of the young ladies that used it. They arrived from Swindon and would congregate in an area to the west of the camp known as Piccadilly, where there were a collection of temporary wooden buildings housing wet canteens, shops, and cafes.

Postcard with flap which when lifted revealed a view of Chiseldon Camp.

Still More

By 1917 it was clear that hospital provision was again insufficient, and the Director of the Wiltshire Red Cross asked whether a new hospital could be built in Swindon. The council obliged, and offered to pay the rent on the Wesleyan Institute on Faringdon Road, if it could be converted into an appropriate site. However, the Army Council declined the council's offer, preferring instead to take over a section of the workhouse at Stratton. Although this, of course, had certain negative connotations, with the normal inhabitants being the broken and destitute, it provided a peaceful place for recovering soldiers, with its countryside location and plenty of space for exercise and relaxation. The only slight drawback of the location was the distance from the main town, which meant that, at first, many of the gifts and visitors to the patients were not from Swindon. This changed, however, as the townsfolk got used to

A blessing taking place in Town Gardens, with an ambulance car in the foreground.

seeing the 'hospital blue' around the place, and the usual enthusiastic support for the place grew, with visits from Swindonians as
well as local orchestras, concerts, exhibitions, and special sales all
being organised to help. There was also the medical staff, mostly
of the Red Cross, and many of them local too. Despite the horror
of some of the injuries, and the fact that staff may had suffered
losses themselves, the nurses gave up not just weeks or months,
but years of their lives to support the wounded. To paraphrase
Bavin's description, 'this devoted band of workers stood to their
posts, to lighten the sufferings of others with unflagging energy'.

After the armistice, on 19 December 1918, a Christmas supper
and dance was organised at the hospital in Stratton, at which all
staff and patients received a present. A letter sent to the hospital
by Corporal Jason Brooks of the Royal Engineers expresses what
such hospitality meant to a wounded soldier: 'Please accept
my best thanks for your great kindness in thinking of me this
Christmas by way of a gift. I'm very proud of it, and have shown
it around to my chums here to let them see that a Tommy is not
easily forgotten down Swindon way.'

4

KEEPING THE HOME FIRES BURNING

For many families the man was the only breadwinner. As a consequence, the war's need for men presented many painful choices. On the one hand, men of serving age were expected to join up and at the beginning of the war that is exactly what most men wanted to do. On the other hand, it often meant leaving the family in potential strife. In the early days, with expectations of a short conflict, volunteers were abundant, but as time went on fewer and fewer men were willing to make the leap and sign up.

More and More Men

The 'Derby Scheme' allowed men to voluntarily 'attest' to join up at some later point. Unfortunately, such was the need for men that the scheme started to run out of volunteers early in 1916. Furthermore, the scheme was flawed in that it called up men by age group, meaning that married men engaged in important work at home were being called up while single men in unimportant occupations were not. Consequently, in January 1916, conscription arrived, and with it the inevitable difficulties of enforcement. On 9 February, Swindon Town Council appointed a tribunal and by 21 February it was in session, hearing cases of those who felt they could not to go to war. The tribunal's records show that the cases were usually extremely deserving; for example, a 38-year-old bricklayer

A young Joseph Edwards (who was later killed in action), posing with his mother outside their house on Percy Street.

with a sick 73-year-old mother and no other family nearby; a 26-year-old grocer who had invested all his money in a new business which would fail because his wife had a baby to look after; a widower who had to make the meals for his three children; and a widowed mother who appealed for her son not to be sent away. 'Oh, don't you take him from me, gentlemen,' she pleaded, 'I shall be left all alone.'

Inevitably, many of the cases for exemption related to the fitness of the applicant, and the line between medically fit and unfit was never easily defined. At first, the medical aptitude of applicants was determined by a complex series of categories, A, B1, C1, C2, C3 etc., though this was simplified in December 1917 to four grades: Grade I was considered to be a normal standard of health and strength; men of Grade II could stand a 'fair' amount of physical strain and had reasonable sight and hearing; while those of Grade III would not be suitable for combatant service, but might be fit for clerical or other sedentary work; and Grade IV, meant totally unfit for any form of military service. Despite best efforts to categorise levels of fitness, decisions were made by the medical examiner, usually civilians employed by the Medical Board. With payment based on the number of applicants dealt with, the process could easily become arbitrary and, in some cases, health checks were not made at all, with men being determined as fit by a cursory glance. It was no wonder that there was often uncertainty about who was and who was not fit. In 1914, the Swindon press printed an apparent clarification from the Local Government Board:

Harold Robins, an Air Mechanic 1st class in the Royal Naval Air Service, was killed in an air attack on 19 October 1917.

ONLY THOSE 'USEFUL TO THE ARMY' WANTED

The Local Government Board issues the following announcement:–
There appears to be some misapprehension with regard to an Army Council instruction recently issued as to men in medical categories B3 or C3.

The instruction was issued to recruiting officers, and directed that for the present men in the medical categories in question are not to be called up or posted unless they are clerks or are following a trade useful to the Army.

So far as tribunals are concerned, they should deal with the cases of men in these medical categories in the ordinary course on their merits in accordance with the directions already issued to them.

In any case in which exemption is not justified and is therefore refused, the men will be available for the Army if they should be required, or may be used as substitutes.

Like elsewhere, Swindon also had a share of people who simply didn't believe in war. Known as conscientious objectors, or 'conchies', they were people who refused to take an active part in the war for religious, moral, or political reasons. The tribunal does not record a large number of such applications, but occasionally such 'perplexing cases' did arise, such as William Robins, who was described as a conscientious objector and activist. William had two brothers in the forces, one of whom, Harold Richard Robins, served as an Air Mechanic 1st Class in the Royal Naval Air Service. Harold was stationed at Dunkirk Naval Air Station where he was killed in an air attack on 19 October 1917. Despite this, or perhaps because of it, his brother William stood by his pacifist beliefs throughout the war, and went on to became Mayor of Swindon in 1932.

The tribunal, in an effort to avoid being unduly harsh while also fulfilling its duty, tried to be as fair as possible and take each case on its individual merits. Sometimes the outcome of the hearings would be to task the applicant with a job of equal importance to joining the military, such as farm work; sometimes it would impose a £2 fine, and hand the applicant over to the military as an absentee. In one recorded case, the applicant (whose name is not known) applied for exemption on the grounds that, as a firm adherent to the beliefs of Leo Tolstoy, he could not take an oath to kill anyone. After considerable discussion and arguments held in secret, the tribunal eventually granted conditional exemption.

Overall, whether the applicant was objecting on moral grounds, or had practical or emotional needs, the tribunal was firm. Exemptions were usually only a temporary reprieve, with men being given a few weeks, or months if they were lucky, before they were conscripted. The only exceptions were carriers of a 'pink card', issued by an employer to denote that a worker's services were indispensable.

Consequently, ever greater numbers of men found themselves going off to war, leaving their families in danger of dire financial situations. In an attempt to deal with such difficulties, the Prince of Wales inaugurated a national fund for the relief of distress. On 7 August, the Mayor of Swindon held a large meeting of representative citizens in the Town Hall and an executive committee and sub-committees were formed, as well as a subscription list. After just a fortnight, £675 10s 9d had been raised and the accounts show that by the end of 1915, £3,345 9s 11½d had been donated, with 1,983 registered cases of people in need.

However, against expectations, as 1915 got underway, many Swindon businesses enjoyed considerable economic prosperity; although the cost of living rose, many employers were able to offer bonuses to their staff to help them keep their heads above water. This was on an understanding that the bonuses would only be given until 'normal conditions' returned. Things changed, however, as hopes of decisive summer victories faded in that year, and the town's people realised that they needed to consider a longer term approach to war conditions. Local employers rose to the challenge, offering help to the families of servicemen right from the start. The biggest employer, the GWR, supplemented service pay and separation-allowances of men in their employment who had signed up, and they also guaranteed their jobs on return. This was no mean feat given that by September 1914, some 4,000 men had been released from the GWR, many of them from Swindon. In line with the GWR's generous approach, the town council provided half-wages to their employees in the services. The local education committee gave full pay (minus military allowance) to teachers who joined up, with service under the colours being considered as service to the committee.

The Cost of Living

Helping those in need at home was a running battle with ever-increasing costs for food, fuel and other essentials, despite the Board of Trade's early attempts to regulate prices of major necessities. In May 1916, the Board's annual returns showed that prices in general had risen 23 per cent over the year, but that at least food products, particularly fruit and vegetables, were still available in relatively normal quantities. However, over that year, meat and fish prices rose by 30 per cent; sugar and potatoes by 50 per cent; and milk and tea by as much as 25 per cent. Fortunately not everything was affected in the same way, with flour prices only rising by 4 per cent, and bread being a relatively reasonable 7 per cent dearer. Nonetheless, as the year went on, the real effects of war started to show. In January 1916, the local Co-operative Society's stores had managed to drop the price of a 4lb loaf of bread, from 8½*d* to 8*d* and then to 7½*d*, but by September prices were back up again as overall commodity prices started to rise rapidly. The changes were so steep that it was estimated that, since the start of the war, a working-family's household costs had risen by 55 per cent. The problem intensified as food supply chains began to dry up, or produce was diverted towards the war effort, and traders increased prices (sometimes to cover the new costs, sometimes with an unscrupulous eye for extra profit). British meat prices rose by 50 per cent; foreign meat up to 80 per cent; fish almost doubled in price (perhaps due to Swindon being so far from the sea); flour jumped by 70 per cent; and sugar prices rose a staggering 152 per cent above those of May the previous year. Unsurprisingly, people objected to price rises and accusations of profiteering were common. The grocers and other merchants however, were 'very wrath' about such suggestions, and pointed out with some determination that they were only raising prices because wholesale prices had risen. In some cases they even claimed that they were losing money on products because of contracts being cancelled due to the war.

In the stormy conditions that dominated the last quarter of 1914, the 'Picture Palace' in Chiseldon was completely destroyed. The establishment had been built by Alfred Manners, who owned the Empire Theatre, to entertain troops at Chiseldon Camp.

Inevitably, limited supplies meant a drop in quality as well as quantity, with people having to cope with changing standards. For example, in September 1916 the shortage of beef, mutton and pork led to a licence being granted to a slaughterhouse on Stratton Road to provide horse meat for human consumption. As flour supplies shrank, more and more 'substances' were added to flour for the making of 'War Bread', including the rougher elements of grain, as well as maize, barley, rice, peas, beans or potatoes. The *Swindon Advertiser* published the following orders:

- Bread must not be sold until it has been made at least 12 hours.
- The only loaves allowed are the tin loaf, the one-piece oven-bottom loaf, pan-Coburg shape, and twin-sister brick loaf, and rolls weighing not less than 1oz. and not more than 2oz.
- No current, sultana, or milk bread may be made.
- All bread must be sold by weight. All loaves must be 1lb. Or an even number of pounds.
- No wheat, rye, rice, tapioca, sago, manioc, or arrowroot, or produce thereof may be used except for human food.
- No bread or other product of cereals mentioned above must be wasted.

By 1917, bakers were keeping their ingredients secret, perhaps unsurprising given that up to 25 per cent of the make-up of their loaves was officially not regarded as food product.

Bindon's boot-repairing depot was essential as the price of leather rose due to military requirements.

Staff of the Kingshill Co-op with their 'hygienic' delivery vehicles.

The difficulty in digesting such poor quality was blamed for an epidemic of sores breaking out on people's bodies, especially among children, with doctors advising less consumption of bread and more of vegetables.

Price increases also affected most other things. For example, before the war a good pair of men's boots, 'well finished and neat in appearance', could command anything up from 12s 6d, with women's boots about 15s. But almost from the start, the Swindon and District Boot and Leather Trades Association was concerned about rising prices, with military needs having an adverse impact on normal trade. By the end of the war, prices for leather had tripled, and the association drew up new price schedules to pass cost increases on to their customers for both new footwear and repairs.

Meanwhile, price rises and limits were imposed on fuel, with the price of coal rising by several shillings in the first year. Even the GWR, which normally offered generous deals for its staff, had to increase its coal prices for employees up to 25s per ton in March 1916, and 27s 6d by June. Electricity was also affected by rising costs, meaning that lighting was limited. This was made worse by restrictions imposed due to the threat of air attacks. Germany had made all sorts of ominous threats about the capability of its Zeppelins to reach all parts of Britain, and Swindon prepared itself for the worse, expecting at any time to hear the six blasts of the Works hooter which would signify an impending attack. On several occasions the warning was indeed given, when news of nearby raids was heard. Thankfully, although some people swore they saw Zeppelins above, Swindon escaped unharmed, though the unlit streets did nothing to help a darkening atmosphere. Of course things were only going to get worse.

The Price of Beef

By the end of 1917 it was clear that rationing was inevitable. Sure enough, after a winter of long queues outside the shops throughout the cold winter months, the town suffered 'Meatless Sunday' as the butchers all ran out. The town council had no choice but to create a plan to ration essentials, and began with a plea for people to limit themselves, especially in regard to the rarest commodities, like meat and margarine. For a few weeks at the start of the year, margarine brought into the town by the Maypole Company was still issued to schools, but most people seemed incapable of limiting themselves to the suggested figures of 4oz per person per week, so rationing was introduced. As part of the Swindon Tea, Butter and Margarine Scheme of 1918, food cards were printed and distributed, with some blank spaces to allow for other foods that might soon be rationed. At the end of January, every household received its card with the following circular:

In August 1915, Queensland Government, Australia, sent twenty-five quarters of beef and twenty-five carcasses of mutton to Swindon. The meat was distributed from the Swindon Cold Storage and Ice Company by the Butchers' Association, to seventy-one families, with weekly portions of up to 5lbs.

Borough of Swindon, Food Control Committee
Rationing Scheme for Beef, Mutton and Pork

In order to avoid queues, and to secure an equitable distribution of the meat supplies, the Food Control Committee have decided to bring a Rationing Scheme into operation at once.

Herewith is a Ration Card for your household.

You are to state on this card the number of persons living in your house, including lodgers, or boarders, giving those over 14 years of age, and those of 14 years of age and under separately. A household may take out its weekly ration entirely in pork or entirely in beef and mutton, or partly in beef and partly in mutton (if the butcher having regard to his supplies can make it convenient to supply it in this way), but a person who desires pork must take the whole week's ration in pork.

This week you should take the coupon dated 2nd February to your butcher on Friday. If he can supply you on that date he will. If not, you should be able to obtain your supplies on Saturday.

In subsequent weeks you should take your coupon to your butcher at the time you make your purchase.

The ration is 12ozs. for adults and 6ozs. for children of 14 years of age and under.

Having deposited your first coupon with your butcher, you must continue to obtain your weekly supplies from him, unless your coupon is transferred to another butcher by the Committee. You cannot change your butcher yourself, but when you desire to take your week's ration in pork you should take your coupon not later than Thursday morning, to a butcher who deals in pork.

The Committee may at any time transfer your Ration Card from one butcher to another.

The ration may be varied from time to time by the Committee, according to the supplies of meat available.

Town Hall, 29 January 1918

By March, a national scheme had come into force and by July, rations were applied to lard, bacon and sugar too. The need for sugar was not simply because people had a sweet tooth, it was

Ration card issued to a home on Radnor Street.

actually essential to preserve fruit. Without it, locally grown crops, such as apples, pears, strawberries and loganberries, would have rotted.

Throughout the year, most other commodities also suffered shortages and, as well as rationing, prices continued to rise despite the official efforts to keep things within reason. By the end of the summer, people had had enough. One man, a 'navvy' working on the railways who was described as 'a Hercules for size and strength' pushed through the crowd in the Food Controller's office and shouted, 'I say, Boss, am I a babby?' After agreement that he, indeed, did not look much like a baby, the man thrust a scrap of meat across the desk demanding to know 'What's the good of that to me?' According to Bavin, the controller gave the man a supplementary ration for heavy workers fearing that if he did not help the goliath he might well end up as part of his ration himself.

On 28 September, the workers of the GWR issued a message urging their Unions 'to take immediately such steps as are necessary to warn the local Food Control Committee that no further increases in the price of essential commodities will be tolerated'. The workers also hinted that they would take any action needed, 'no matter how drastic, to combat the ever-growing evil of profiteering'. The following week, two brass bands led a procession of workers (estimated to be as many as 10,000 strong) to the town hall, where speakers were met with cheers or cries of 'Shame!' depending on their views. These sorts of protests, which were starting to happen elsewhere too, were a cause of major anxiety for the authorities, saved only by the fact that the war came to an end before they got out of hand.

Time, Gentlemen, Please!

The difficulties of rationing and price rises affected every part of life, including the sale of alcohol. Because of the huge numbers of troops arriving in the town from the very start of the war, limits on drinking were imposed very early on, primarily through controls on the opening and closing times of public houses. But restrictions on how much liquor each person could consume could cause confusion. For example, it was illegal for a man to 'treat' someone else to a drink. Strictly speaking, this meant a man could not actually buy a drink for his wife! By 1918, the situation had deteriorated and Swindon suffered what was referred to as 'an unwonted experience': a beer famine. Throughout the year, from Easter onwards, public houses across the borough were closed on a regular basis. One landlord, perhaps with a hint of sarcasm, put up a notice saying: 'Closed, no beer: God Save the King.'

Still serving beer in a quiet Stanley Street Working Men's Club.

FOR KING AND EMPIRE

The motto of the Empire Theatre was of course, 'the show must go on', and it was driven by Director Alfred Manners, who filled the theatre with a full programme as the war got under way. There were even special late-night trains run to towns and villages as far afield as Trowbridge, Melksham, Faringdon, Ludgershall, and Marlborough, with all the stations in between. The audiences still had standards though. When *Now We Know* was put on, one journalist said: 'One fears that theatre-goers are becoming just a little tired of these American productions.' He further reported that, at the preview, the reception was 'friendly, if not enthusiastic'.

Alfred Manners not only provided entertainment for those at home, he also put huge effort into charitable works and fundraising. Right from the start, on 16 August 1914, Manners started a series of Sunday concerts to raise money for the Prince of Wales National Benefit Fund. As well as arranging for troops to be ferried from Chiseldon Camp to the Empire, Manners also built a 'picture house' at Chiseldon. Sadly, it did not get off to a good start when a terrible storm on 1 December 1914 completely flattened the hastily built building.

Manners' efforts continued throughout the war, with him establishing the 'Christmas Pudding Fund' in 1915, donating £767 8s 2d to the mayor's appeal to send help to local men who had been taken prisoners of war, and raising money for the St Mary's Hostel for Women War Workers via the Swindon Girls' Club Union. In November 1918, a collection organised by Manners raised £258 12s 11d for the Red Cross Society, including takings from a matinee at the theatre, collections at local cinema houses, flag-sales, and subscriptions. On Armistice night in 1918, the Empire was filled with forces men and Manners was publicly thanked for his amazing fundraising and general support for the war effort.

The Empire kept up its publicity in the Swindon press throughout the war.

The audience pose for a photograph outside the Empire Theatre following the show.

A Cheerier Side of Life

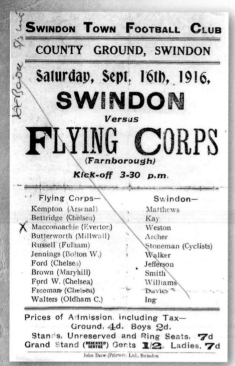

SWINDON TOWN FOOTBALL CLUB

COUNTY GROUND, SWINDON

Saturday, Sept. 16th, 1916,

SWINDON

Versus

FLYING CORPS

(Farnborough)

Kick-off 3-30 p.m.

Flying Corps—	Swindon—
Kempton (Arsenal)	Matthews
Bettridge (Chelsea)	Kay
Macconnachie (Everton)	Weston
Butterworth (Millwall)	Archer
Russell (Fulham)	Stoneman (Cyclists)
Jennings (Bolton W.)	Walker
Ford (Chelsea)	Jefferson
Brown (Maryhill)	Smith
Ford W. (Chelsea)	Williams
Freeman (Chelsea)	Davies
Walters (Oldham C.)	Ing

Prices of Admission, including Tax—
Ground, 4d. Boys 2d.
Stands, Unreserved and Ring Seats, 7d
Grand Stand (RESERVED CENTRE) Gents 1/2, Ladies, 7d

John Drew (Printers) Ltd., Swindon

Swindon Town takes on the Flying Corps as part of war entertainment.

The troubles of war dominated everything, but just as the troops were able to find humour to endure their terrible suffering, the people at home also created ways to bring a bit of light-heartedness into their lives. Inevitably, much of the focus still revolved around the war, with a predominance of entertainment (concerts, parties, picnics, etc.) arranged specifically to raise funds. But that didn't stop people enjoying themselves, particularly in the early days of the war, when the whole town was filled with an air of excitement and anticipation of something glorious.

However, as the war progressed, moods changed. In the Works, it was announced that there would be no annual trip – a week's holiday arranged by the GWR for the workers and their families – although bonus schemes and individual holidays were offered in its place. Outside the town, while agricultural shows continued with enthusiasm, the pleasure fairs that were normally part of them soon faded away, apart from, in 1918, a flower and vegetable show arranged with a silver cup and two silver salvers up for grabs. Nonetheless, although celebrations and entertainment in general dropped off, considerable efforts were still put into activities for those who really needed a bit of cheering up. This is perhaps exemplified by the mayor's busy diary on Christmas Day 1915:

9.30 a.m. – Taking breakfast to old folk at Sanford Street Congregational School

12 noon – Workhouse (inmates still deserve their Christmas treat)

1.00 p.m. – Children's homes at Stratton

1.30 p.m. – Victoria Hospital

4.00 p.m. – GWR hospital

5.00 p.m. – Olive House children's home

and then – Soldiers' Rest, Newport Street

Meanwhile, the Christmas concert at the Arcadia picture house went ahead as usual, as did Swindon's traditional Christmas football matches against Reading. On Christmas Day itself, victory went to Reading, beating Swindon 4–3. But revenge came on Boxing Day when, in what was described as a hurricane, Swindon won 4–2. Swindon Town also carried on playing throughout the war, often against forces teams, though with no professional players.

Entertaining the Troops

With the huge numbers of troops coming into the town and camped at Chiseldon, Swindon was the natural place to relax when given leave. Throughout the war, an endless swarm of men filled Victoria Road on Saturdays and Sundays, looking for some light relief. As well as the public houses, the men could take in a show at the Empire Theatre or the Electra Palace picture house, which included films such as *The Count* starring Charlie Chaplin. Troops could also take refuge at the YMCA in Fleet Street; have tea or other light refreshments at the Presbyterian church; or enjoy tea, a reading and writing room, and even whist tables, at the Soldiers' Rest in Newport Street, looked after by a Mrs Streeten and her volunteer Ladies' Committee. In one weekend alone in May 1915, 3,000 men passed through the Soldiers' Rest. Sadly, Mrs Streeten's efforts faded after that, following the death of her husband, Dr Streeten. Dr Streeten was the Medical Officer of Health for Swindon.

Poster advertising Charlie Chaplin films at the Electra Palace picture house.

It wasn't just in town that the locals provided activities for the troops. At Chiseldon Camp, the Mayor's Camp Concerts Committee organised regular concerts. There were 161 such concerts arranged between 4 November 1916 and 27 November 1917. Then, after a brief spell where concerts were cancelled because of an outbreak of influenza, another 104 were put on between 17 October 1917 and 18 July 1918. The chairman of the committee, Mr C.K. Warner, had been the leader of the GWR Temperance Choir for some time, and took it upon himself to form a choir with soldiers from the Gloucesters, the Warwicks, the Hampshires and the Cyclist Corps. The choir's first concert was also its last. A week later the men were all in France. Bavin sums up the general gratitude towards efforts to help the men at Chiseldon: 'Many a mother who had never heard of Swindon has cause to bless the Swindon folk who helped her boy to keep up his spirits in the weary camp, and perhaps help him from temptation as well as depression.'

Families

Most of the entertainment during the war was arranged by volunteers. As well as direct entertainments for the men, the needs of the wives and mothers left behind were also considered. It was not long before a committee was created to run 'The Social Club for the Wives and Mothers of Members of the Armed Forces'. The club arranged weekly 'tea-meetings' and they always provided music and songs too, alongside a constant flow of interesting speakers. On occasions, professionals from the Empire Theatre would appear, giving their time voluntarily at special events at the Town Hall, or in the Drill Hall. One councillor, Alderman J. Powell, was particularly keen to help the club, arranging tea parties for members on fourteen occasions in 1917 in Town Gardens. Alderman Powell was known as 'Raggie' due to the fact that he started his career as a rag-and-bone merchant, and became a well-loved character in the town. He engaged the Central Cinema and the theatre for specific events. On one occasion, the club organised a 'tea show' at the Mechanic's Institute where mothers, wives and children were entertained by the 'Wags', and each child received a bag of fruit and sweets donated by the Rifle Club.

Boys at the GWR Works go on strike demanding 'proper' wages.

Of course for parents, life was not simply about entertaining the children. Education was considered extremely important, and a child's truancy from school would usually mean a visit to the court for the parents. John Homer, a chain-smith in the GWR Works, was summoned before the court to answer for his 12-year-old son, Roland, who had only been present at fifty-six attendances out of a possible 111. The magistrate's clerk noted, 'it is disgraceful! He won't even be able to read the regulations for the next war!' And John Rowland, another GWR worker, from the boiler shop, was also summoned in respect of his 13-year-old son, Harry, who had a similar truancy rate. Despite the legal summons usually being addressed to the father, it was generally the mother who answered to the court. Harry's mother told the magistrate's clerk, 'I don't keep him away. I have been ill for the last two years. I have four or five children at school.' To which the clerk replied, 'Four or five? Surely you ought to know exactly how many.' As it turned out, the Rowlands had thirteen children, so perhaps some uncertainty about their whereabouts was understandable. Nonetheless, in both cases, the court fined the families 5s.

As the navy struggled to get enough fresh fruit and vegetables for its men, a national appeal was set up. In a single month, the people of Swindon sent more than 80 tons of food to aid the men on the high seas.

However, for some young people (boys particularly) who had already left school but were below the serving age, the war could mean financial prosperity unheard of before that time. The need to fill spaces left by men who had signed up created a huge demand for young people, and after a strike by boy workers at the GWR Works, who felt they should be paid appropriately, wages rose accordingly. Though, as with most aspects of life, this was a double-edged sword, as the local court records show. On the one hand, there were those like William Henry Mason, who was described as a 'rough-looking youth' and was charged after being found asleep in a lavatory near the Whale Bridge. On the other hand, one young lad who was arrested for riding a bike after dark without lights revealed that he was earning 35s working at a munitions factory – that was seven times more than many of the adult women in employment. For the very young, success did not come so readily. At a Baby Show held in Town Gardens over 500 babies entered. It was not an easy day for the judges.

5

A WOMEN'S WAR

As the previous chapter discussed, the core problem facing families in 1914 was the reliance on men to provide the family income, and it was men who went to war. In theory, military pay should have covered costs for the family at home. In practice, this was not the case, with military salaries being insufficient to cover the soldiers' costs abroad and leave enough to send home, if they actually sent home anything at all. The solution to this was provided by the women of Swindon.

In Swindon, the bulk of the male working-population was employed in the Works (in 1908 it was estimated that 80 per cent of the male working-population worked there). As many of these headed to France, female worker numbers increased in the GWR Works, although initially it was reported that difficulties arose because of the inadequate toilet and canteen facilities, and because many of the men worked while stripped to the waist. At the time it was considered inappropriate for women to work under such conditions. Nonetheless, the numbers of female railway workers increased in 1915, particularly the numbers of clerks. This was due to a massive increase in documentation and accounting that related to work being done specifically for the war effort. By 1916 there were enough ladies in one of the accounts areas for group photographs to be taken. To promote the need for, and importance of, women at work, the Ministry of Munitions used an image of women in one of Swindon's large machine workshops as the cover of their sales and instructions literature.

Kate 'Kit' North (front right), sitting with her uniformed worker colleagues. Kit's brother Albert was in the Royal Field Artillery.

As the war progressed, the need for workers on war business meant further employment opportunities for women. In June 1916, the government took over the Imperial Tobacco Company's factory for the Ministry of Munitions, and many of the girls who were hoping for work with the tobacco company were taken on for the production of munitions instead, for the lowly wage of 5s a week. In 1916, another munitions factory was opened on land between Gorse Hill and Stratton, specifically bought for the purpose by the War Office. Around the same time, J. Gundry and Co. opened a small factory to create ropes and nets. In both cases, the factories were staffed almost exclusively by women. Known as 'Powder Factories', the munitions works paid higher wages to the women, for the dangerous and filthy job of filling shells with explosives.

Nursing the Wounds

It was not just in taking up men's jobs at home that women helped the war effort. There were also specific wartime roles, such as 'leaving their homes, their leisure, and their sports, in order to become proficient in the art of nursing'. From 1917, the Women's Army Auxiliary Corps provided 57,000 female members at home and abroad, after Field Marshall Haig promoted the idea that women could play an invaluable part in the war in France. In Swindon, women rallied to this call just as they did everywhere else. Within a week of the start of the war, the Red Cross Society had organised itself, formed two Voluntary Aid Detachments and raised the first £303 of many thousands collected during the war.

Under the watchful eyes of Miss E.B. Walker of the Victoria Hospital, and Miss Dismorr of Wroughton, practical training of nurses began (*see* Chapter 3: Work of War). Before long it was realised that a dedicated hospital was necessary, and the GWR Baths on Milton Road were taken over for that purpose under the management of Miss C. Deacon. At the time, of course, no one knew just how long the war would last, with enthusiasm based on a notion that victory was only a matter of weeks away. Nonetheless, as the months turned to years, the numbers of wounded increased and the women themselves suffered their own losses. But the work of local nurses was unflagging, as were the 'less skilled' tasks of sewing, cleaning, cooking, motor-driving, fetching and carrying, and the all-important raising of funds. At the end of the war, three local women were particularly noted for their dedication: Miss Rose, the Honorary Secretary of the Red Cross Society, and Mrs Muir and Sister Whistler, who were both awarded the Royal Red Cross. These women were simply representing the many women who had been involved, with an overall commendation that 'Wounded men who were fortunate enough to be sent to Swindon will always have in their hearts a warm corner for the town because of the devotion and loving service shown by so many of Swindon's women'.

But nursing was just the tip of the iceberg. Bavin describes women's new roles in wartime and although his words echo the patronising attitude towards women of that time, he does give some idea of the breadth and depth of a dramatically changing society:

> But in this war women were not content with nursing only; they found their way into many branches of trade and into many professions; they were found in the office, behind the counter, on the land, at the bench, delivering the letters, in fact in a thousand and one places where years before people would have declared it was impossible for a woman to work; but there they were, cheerful and efficient, enabling the country to 'carry on' when it seemed that all her workers were wanted for fighters. How familiar the neat uniforms of the WAAC, WREN and WRAF have become! The women of these corps were willing even to go to Flanders to work in aerodromes and other workshops, 'doing their bit' by assisting in building aeroplanes, making and filling shells, and making munitions. Others felt drawn to the land, and so one saw the 'land girl', dressed in her smock and leather leggings, driving in her market-cart to town, or in charge of a drove of cattle.

By the end of the war, women had taken on roles in nearly all aspects of the town's economy, in the factories, running shops and businesses, dealing with all manner of administration, and working on the land. In March 1917, the shortage of men led to women being given jobs as tram conductors which, up to that point, had been a male-only occupation, and, by the end of that year 'girl-clerks' were also being employed by the town council. In response to the need for women in these new roles, the Education Committee offered full training for a range of employment skills for women, including typewriting, shorthand, and business methods. Nonetheless, such professional schemes were often aimed at educated women, and it was extremely unlikely for a worker's wife with small children to be able to take advantage of them if her husband had joined up.

The Education Committee also had to turn to women to fill a gap in the numbers of teachers. The shortage was so bad that elsewhere schools had to resort to only teaching half the pupils at any given time, leaving the rest to 'roam the streets'. The problem was that teacher training was a long process and filling the gap with untrained staff was not considered sufficient. As a consequence in Swindon, a call was made to women who had been teachers before leaving the profession to start a family, as was common at that time. The response was so strong that, once again, Swindon's women solved the problem. In many cases the woman kept records of their time, often written in beautiful copperplate script in marbling-decorated diaries,

Working on the trams changed from being a male-only profession as the war went on.

Lily (front right) who lived in Dixon Street, with her munitions worker colleagues.

examples of which are kept at the Wiltshire &
Swindon History Centre. The diaries talk of
classrooms heated by wood fires, children regularly weighed and measured, and classes being
closed down during sickness epidemics. During
the war, children were also given special holidays
for blackberry picking, sliding in icy weather or
even tea parties.

A sewing class started at
the Methodist Hall in 1915.
It was led by Mrs Elsie
Ball, and established to
raise funds for the war
effort. However, such was
its success that it carried
on for another fifty years,
making clothing and
household items to help
other good causes.

Comforts for the Wiltshires

Those women who did not actually join up, or were
not employed, still played a large and essential part
through voluntary and unpaid work, both directly
and indirectly helping efforts at the front. As the war drew on,
it was clear that more work at home was needed to help individual
troops. In December 1916, the Red Cross Society was made
responsible for providing necessities for prisoners of war, but for
most soldiers there were more day-to-day needs that the army
seemed unable to provide for. At the beginning of autumn 1914,
an appeal was made to Swindon's mayor by Lady Heytesbury,
for people to help the local regiment, the Wiltshires. As a consequence, ladies of the Prince of Wales' Relief Fund Committee
formed a special subcommittee designated to provide 'Comforts
for the Wiltshire Regiment'. Led by local women Mary Slade and
Kate Handley, the group's purpose was to raise funds and make or
buy woollen goods to be sent to the men at the front in Flanders,
and at military camps both at home and abroad.

Within weeks, packages of gloves, socks, body-belts, scarves,
jerseys, helmets (balaclavas) and other articles were despatched
to Devizes to be forwarded to the front. Every Thursday,
a large pile of packages was mounted at the Town Hall ready
for despatch. All the articles were produced by women, and the
management and organising of this 'cottage industry' was a
women-only affair too. In fact, the only exceptions were several
men drafted in to help with some of the heavy packing work.
In many instances, children sent notes with the goods, sometimes designating a parcel to 'A brave soldier', or 'To one who

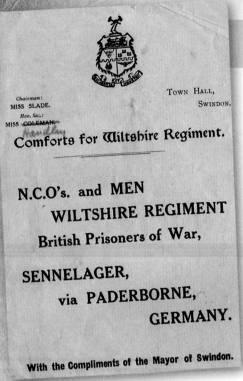

Label for a parcel being sent to prisoners of war of the Wiltshire Regiment.

has received no Christmas present'. Responses from soldiers suggest that some of the knitters may have been young girls: 'Writing a few lines to thank you for your kind gift, and I must say your father and your mother are quite proud of you, and I am quite proud of you too.'

In total, the Comforts Committee sent: 5,229 pairs of socks, 2,473 scarves, 1,452 pairs of mittens, 880 helmets, 238 belts and 901 kneecaps. Also, through their fundraising efforts, the women were able to send thirty-two footballs as well as many games and, of course, very large quantities of tobacco and cigarettes.

Beyond the items sent through the local committee, countless other things were sent through national organisations, or personally. The local press noted that the numbers of articles and success of subscriptions was only part of the story, as 'this does not indicate the zeal of the women of the town of all classes and all ages, who are most eager to assist'. Though the men were not to be excluded, with one pair of socks received that were 'splendidly knitted by a fellow-comrade'. We can only hope he took the advice laid down by the committee for those creating their own packages: 'All socks should be washed before being sent.'

The Rape of Belgium

Swindon's women did not limit themselves to helping their own men. At the outset of the war, the Germans dismissed the 1839 Treaty of London (which guaranteed Belgium neutrality) and engaged in a campaign against the Belgian population and its property. It is estimated that some 6,000 Belgians were killed and 1.5 million had to flee from their country, with many coming to England. In September 1914, Swindon's 'Liberal Women' organised for over 500 items of clothing to be sent to London for the refugees, and many households in the town and surrounding villages were offered up as 'Belgian Homes'. About thirty homes were equipped through loans and gifts of furniture, money, food and clothing as refugees started arriving in the town, initially being housed in the Vicar of Swindon's house on Bath Road.

> Swindon's women, led by Mrs T. Arkell of the local brewery family, collected 161,651 eggs for the wounded during the war, making Swindon the eleventh highest number out of 2,000 depots across the country.

The refugees, many of whom were peasants, arrived with tales of hunger, anguish and terror, and included a 5-year-old girl 'whose arm bore the cruel gash of a German sabre'. In response, Swindon looked after over 350 Belgians, and huge efforts were made to raise funds by the various women-run committees. Although eventually the local committee had to turn to the Central War Refugee Fund for help, through most of the war the people of Swindon looked after their guests unaided, raising nearly £6,000 over the whole period.

Funds were primarily generated through events, with the first Belgian 'Flag-Day' fete being held in Town Gardens on 28 August 1915. The event had music, gymnastic displays, songs, games and dancing, and was to start a pattern of events which included concerts at the Mechanics' Institute, picnics, fairs, bazaars, and private parties such as those organised by the Workers' Educational Association at the Higher Elementary School, with cello solos by Professor Hollebeke, songs by Belgian and English singers, and a song composed by Alfred Williams and translated into French. Later in 1915, with donations of tools and equipment, a workshop was created allowing Belgians to create fine furniture and wooden toys, many of which were sold through the Christmas Bazaar of local traders, McIlroys.

Swindon's commitment to the Belgians was recognised at the end of the war, with King Albert conferring the 'Medaille de la Reine Elizabeth' on three of the main women behind the Belgian refugee committee: Mrs Arnold-Forster, Mrs Tanner and Mrs Tindle.

SCHOOL
BROTHERHOOD

The Great War was no respecter of family ties, and tragedy often struck more than once for Swindon families. Nowhere is this more evident than on the 1936 memorial to former pupils of Sanford Street School, where no less than seven sets of brothers are listed amongst the 130 war dead from this single school, in both army and navy.

Horace Corser, aged 25, was killed on 11 January 1918, while serving with the 79th Field Company, Royal Engineers. His older brother, Reginald, had died two years earlier on 31 May 1916, while serving as an engine room artificer on HMS *Defence* at the Battle of Jutland – the largest sea clash of the war, fought between the colossal Royal Navy Grand Fleet and the Imperial German Navy's High Seas Fleet. Another Old Sandfordian, Arthur Barnes, died on the same day during the same battle. Arthur was an ordinary signalman on board HMS *Queen Mary*, aged only 18. His younger brother, William, joined the 2nd Battalion of the Wiltshire Regiment, and was killed in action at the Battle of Arras the following year.

The Leggett brothers, William and Earnest, joined up in Swindon at the same time, going on to see action with the 1st Battalion, Wiltshire Regiment on the Ypres Salient. On 16 June 1915, William was shot through the stomach, with the bullet exiting through his hip, and taken into a dugout where his brother stayed with him until he died. Earnest wrote home to their mother: 'He was a very brave chap and was very happy, right up to the last. I was proud of the way he stuck it out.' Sadly, Earnest himself was killed in action less than three months later.

SANFORD STREET SCHOOL
1914 — 1918

ANDERSON H.	DRURY W.	LAWES G.	SCHOFIELD S.
BAKER E.	DUCK E.	LEGG W.	SCULL P.
BAKER F.	DULIN W.	LEGGETT E.	SEAGER H.
BARNES A.	ELLIS C.	LEGGETT W.	SEAGER H. J.
BARNES W.	EMERY S.	LOVE G.	SEAGER J.
BEARD F.	GEORGE H.	LUCAS T.	SEAGER P.
BECKETT H.	GILLARD S.	LYNES N.	SHARLAND J.
BICK C.	GLASS A.	MANT F.	SINGER H.
BIRKS O.	GREEN E.	MARKS C.	SMITH C.
BRITTAIN H.	GRIFFIN P.	MATTHEWS S.	SMITH G. A.
BOWEN E.	GRIFFIN M.	MATTHEWS W.	SMITH S.
BRADLEY H.	GUNN E.	MATTOCK F.	SOUTHWELL H.
BURT C.	HACKER A.	MAYO T.	STINCHCOMBE E.
BUTCHER A.	HAGGARD S.	MILES R.	TAVENER P.
CANNINGS E.	HAMMOND S.	MINETT J.	TAYLOR R.
CHAPMAN W.	HARRISON A.	MUTTON E.	THOMAS W. H.
CLAPHAM F.	HARTLEY H.	NASH G.	TOWNSEND R.
CLIFFORD G.	HINDER P.	O'CONNELL D.	WARD J.
COLES C.	HINTON G. C.	PIDGEON G.	WHATLEY F.
COOK W.	HINTON G. E.	POOLE B.	WHETHAM C.
CORBETT A.	HODGES P.	PREATER A.	WHETHAM J.
CORBETT C.	HUMPHRIES L.	PREATER C.	WHITE E. G.
CORSER H.	JEFFORD L.	PREATER H.	WILLIAMS A.
CORSER R.	JEW A.	PROBETS T.	WILLIAMS E. A.
CREBER S.	JOHNSEY L.	PROBETS W.	WILLIAMS E. J.
CROCKETT R.	JOHNSTON C.	REVELEY V.	WILLIAMS H.
DEAN F.	JONES F.	RICKETTS P.	WILLIAMS T.
DENTON W.	JONES F. G.	ROBERTS C.	WINCHURST B.
DIXON E.	KETHERO C.	ROBINSON F.	WINCHURST S.
DIXON N.	KNEE D.	ROWLAND E.	WINCHURST W.
DREW F.	LAMBOURNE H.	SALOWAY W.	WINSLOW J.
DREWITT S.	LANG C.	SANSOM F.	WOODHAM J.

William and Earnest Leggett, who served with the 1st Wilts Battalion in the Ypres Salient, and the Sanford Street School roll of honour, now hanging in Radnor Street cemetery chapel.

The Stalwart Mary Slade

As the war progressed, news about the needs of soldiers abroad increased and letters from prisoners of war (POWs) started coming in, in some cases simply begging for bread. In the first half of the war, the Comforts for the Wiltshires scheme was for men from anywhere across the county, but by the end of 1916 the work had become more place-specific, with Swindon women collecting for Swindon men who had been taken prisoner. Inevitably, as the war progressed the number of prisoners rose. For example, on 21 March 1918, the 1st, 2nd and 6th Battalions of the Wiltshires found themselves in the path of the massive German Spring Offensive and, by the end of the carnage, some 200 men from Swindon were taken prisoner on that single day.

Back home, Mary Slade, who had been instrumental in the raising of comforts for front line troops, switched much of her effort to helping POWs, and rallied other women to the cause. Without her, and the aid she managed to raise and send out, there is little doubt that many of the Swindon men would not have come home again.

Mary Slade, who led so much of the help for troops and their families in Swindon throughout the war and beyond.

Born in Bradford on Avon in 1872, Mary Elizabeth Slade moved to Swindon in 1899 to take up a teaching post at King William Street School. Mary led the 'Comforts' committee in the raising of supplies and materials by persuading local shops, schools and residents to contribute, also managing to spend £2 a week initially on groceries that were to be sent to prisoners who were, at that time, known to be receiving nothing more than a bowl of cabbage soup and two slices of dry bread each day. By October 1915 the women were sending food and comfort parcels to 660 men of the Wiltshires, including 332 at Gottingen and 152 at Munster. The parcels were addressed individually, enabling them to find their proper recipients as men were shifted from one camp to another. Each prisoner should have received one of the desperately welcomed packages every seven weeks.

Mary Slade was awarded the MBE for her services during the war. It is now in the Wiltshire & Swindon History Centre.

KRIEGSGEFANGENENSENDUNG

POST CARD

THE ADDRESS TO BE WRITTEN ON THIS SIDE

Hon. SECRETARY,
Wiltshire Regiment Care Committee,
(Swindon Branch.)

Town Hall,
SWINDON,
England.

Postcard from a German prisoner-of-war camp.

Two letters thanking the Comforts committee for the relief they sent.

Group 4.
Scheveningen
Holland.

March 21st 1918

Dear Miss Slade
I dont think I can thank you enough on paper for what you did for me while a prisoner in Germany & Russia but I take this opportunity of thanking you very much. It is a real pleasure to be here in Holland after 3½ years behind barbed wire I trust all the boys will get exchanged very soon I feel very much for my comrades whom I left behind I feel sure their turn will soon come. By the Way Sergt Bull stays in my room from the 2nd Wiltshires he says he knows you. quite well pleased to say we are in good health and very happy. Again Thanking you + your committee I Remain yours Always Grateful
G Mills Sergt

Göttingen.
Hanover.
7-3-15.

Madam,
On behalf of my com-rades of the Wiltshire Regiment, I have been asked to convey to you and to all those connected with the work, our deepest thanks for the parcels of underclothing forward-ed to us

It will probably never be realised with what gladness each parcel is received,
(sd) J. Welsh, Sergt.
2/Wiltshire Regt.

Postcard from Germany to Kate Handley, Hon. Secretary of the Comforts Committee.

At the end of July 1916, Mary's women had despatched 1,365 parcels of groceries, 4,741 loaves of bread, 38 parcels of clothing and 15 stacks of books. In the five months leading up to the end of November 1916, a total of 3,750 parcels had been dispatched. One of the recipients, T. Saddler, said on his return: 'Had it not been for the parcels received out there from Great Britain we should have starved.'

Official recognition of the committee's work came in July 1919, when Mary Slade and Kate Handley were invited to a garden party at Buckingham Palace. Then, in 1920, Mary was awarded the MBE for her war efforts. But that was not the end of her work. In the poverty and hardship that followed the war, Mary continued to raise funds for Swindon families, carrying on right through the Second World War too. Mary Slade died at the age of 87 on 31 January 1960, at her home on Avenue Road. The previous evening she had been a special guest at the Choir Boy's party at Christ Church.

Mothers, Sisters, Daughters and Wives

One of Swindon's women's biggest contributions was their collective response to the hard realities of war. This chapter has glimpsed the many roles that Swindon's women took during the war, but this really is only half the story. As well as taking on all these new areas, the women still had their 'traditional' roles: children still needed bringing up, cleaning and washing still needed to be done and everyday life did not stop because there was a war on. Beyond that, everyone had relatives, close or distant, who were involved directly in the war. Even if there was no direct tragedy, the worry, fear and uncertainty infused every aspect of life. Tragically, of course, for many of Swindon's women their worst fears were realised.

In 1911, the census shows that a lady called Celia Sarah Pitt was living in Rodbourne with her husband William, a boiler-maker and labourer in the GWR Works, and their four children. William, an ex-serviceman, re-enlisted in October 1914 when he was 43 years old and the family now had two further children. After a year and a half of active service, William was permanently discharged from the army, suffering with tuberculosis, which many men contracted during the war. For three months William lived in the garden shed to avoid infecting other members of the family, and for the 'fresh air' which at the time was believed to be beneficial. However, this didn't help, and William died leaving Celia with no income and six children to provide for. Much of the help for women in this sort of terrible situation was provided for by other women, such as Mary Slade's committee, which did not stop at helping front-line troops or POWs. An entry in the committee's minute book for 3 July 1919 reads:

Celia Pitt of Rodbourne was left to look after six children after her army husband died of tuberculosis, the sad fate of many soldiers.

> Help for Mrs MJ Walker, whose husband late of the 1st Somerset Regt and the 1st Wiltshire Regt, is in the Devizes asylum as a result of his war service. A grant of £4:10:0 was made to assist Mrs Walker temporarily on the proposition of Mrs Morris seconded by Miss Gover.

Another entry, dated 9 August 1921, shows how the effects of the war did not go away quickly:

> Mrs E Groves, a widow of the late Sgt William A Groves, Wiltshire Regt, whose pension is 6s per week. She has Poor Law Relief of 12s 6d per week for her two children. She has been very ill and unable to work and is now in great distress until she is well enough to work again. The Committee decided to grant £2 10s for Mrs Groves to be distributed at 10s per week for five weeks by the Hon. Secretary (Kate Handley).

In 1915, Mrs F. Chirgwin and her young son Richard, from Swindon, were second-class passengers on the *Lusitania* when it was sunk by a German torpedo, killing 1,201 passengers.

For women like these, the war broke up family life at the very time when many would have expected, or at least hoped, to be settling down with an employed husband, a home, and children growing up. And of course it was not just the wives who suffered. For every husband lost, there was a broken-hearted mother too. Another Swindon resident, Mary Jane Preater, was married to Charles Preater. He was the owner of a haulage business and the licensee of the New Inn on Cromwell Street where he and Mary lived with their ten children, many of whom were young adults by the time the war came. Consequently, instead of some of the children taking over the businesses and relieving Mary and her husband of some of the burden, four of the six sons signed up. All four went off to war and only one returned. It is impossible to imagine what receiving three such notifications would be like for a parent:

Arthur Benjamin Preater, Private, Wiltshire Regiment, 2nd Battalion.
Killed in action on the 18 October 1916, aged 30.
Charles Lewis Preater, Private, Wiltshire Regiment, 6th Battalion.
Killed in action 29 April 1918, aged 29.
Herbert Frederick Preater, Lance Sergeant, Worcestershire Regiment, 2/8th Battalion.
Killed in action 1 November 1918, aged 22.

Although the youngest of the Preater sons to be killed was 22, many much younger lads were lost. At the end of August 1914, Frank Sutton, son of Albert and Emily Sutton of Purton, enlisted for the Wiltshire Regiment. He was 16 years and 4 months old. Four months later, Frank arrived in France, joining his battalion at the beginning of February 1915, before suffering a series of medical conditions including boils and a chest deformity. But Frank's illnesses did not stop him from seeing action. Over the next two years, according to the *North Wilts Herald*, Frank was gassed at Ypres; sent to Mesopotamia where he caught dysentery; evacuated to India; returned to Mesopotamia to be at the fall of Baghdad in 1917; and, finally, died of wounds received on 30 March 1917. Frank is remembered on the Basra Memorial in Iraq.

Thankfully, there were good news stories too. In June 1916, another 16 year old, Richard Slade (no relation to Mary Slade as far as is known), who was a pupil from King William Street School for boys, managed to persuade the authorities that he was 19 and joined the army. After three months in service, his parents, the school and the army managed to track him down, verify his age and have him sent home again, safe and sound.

Three years after the end of the war, in 1921, the census shows that there were in excess of 1.7 million more females than males in the population of the country. Bavin sums it up:

> This war has been spoken of as a 'Women's War', because never before have the women of the country taken so active a part in the nation's struggle. By the time peace had returned, distribution of jobs by gender has changed forever. Women not only made up huge numbers of the forces, but they worked in every area back home too, 'cheerful and efficient, enabling the country to carry on'.

6

WEST COUNTRY TO WESTERN FRONT

The men of Swindon, like men from all over the country, served in a vast range of different circumstances and conditions, performing an equally vast range of activities and tasks. It is estimated that some 6,000 Swindon men saw service – including the born-and-bred, workers, visitors and those who had moved on to pastures new. However, as Bavin puts it, 'it is impossible to frame a perfectly complete list of the Swindon men who enlisted … in view of the many removals of families from the town and the failure of many to reply to the numerous appeals for names'. In that light, this and the next chapter attempt to give at least a taste of the colossal story that those men wrote.

Swindon 'Pals'

One Swindon soldier described 'how he used to sit admiring the vivid and intensely interesting fire-work display – the exploding shells, the various kinds of signals, such as six lights on a line gently floating across the sky, and the phosphorous and thermite shells, which burst into showers of golden rain'.

The story of 'Pals' regiments in the Great War, where friends, neighbours and colleagues from a single area joined up and served side-by-side, is well known, and it is a tale in which those cities, towns and districts are justifiably proud. Swindon did not have a 'Pals' regiment or unit as such, but it might as well have had. In fact in the lead up to the war, Swindon had four 'Territorial', part-time military units in which groups of Swindon men all served together:

- Swindon Company of the Wilts (Fortress) Royal Engineers
- 'D' Squadron, Royal Wiltshire Yeomanry
- 1st Battery (Wilts) Royal Field Artillery
- 1st Unit of the Wiltshire Royal Army Medical Corps (RAMC) (Territorial)

The following sections give a brief outline of the first three of these units (the RAMC is covered in Chapter 3: Work of War) and at the end of the next chapter there is a small section giving examples of where Swindon men served in other battalions of the Wiltshire Regiment, other forces and in different parts of the world.

The Engineers of War: Swindon Company of the Wilts (Fortress) Royal Engineers

Given the skills of those who worked in the GWR Works, it is no surprise that Swindon had its own unit of Royal Engineers (RE). However, the sophisticated mechanical engineering of the sort needed for railway development was not always what was required in a military context. In wartime the term 'engineering' had a slightly more down-to-earth meaning and Swindon's engineering troops spent most of their time digging ditches, laying water pipes, pouring concrete, spanning rivers, unrolling barbed wire, or erecting wooden huts, often under enemy gunfire. In essence, the engineers' role was to deliver infrastructure to enable the other troops to fight. They built everything from fences to fortresses, hence the name of the Swindon Company of the Wiltshire (Fortress) Royal Engineers. Appropriately, the Swindon RE were at Fort Purbrook in Portsmouth when war was declared in August 1914, and were instantly moved along the coast to work on the Portland defences at Weymouth. At the same time, a second line unit was created back in Swindon, and sent down to join and augment the original unit.

Following intensive training, especially in bridge building and trench digging, the first line unit was sent to France in January 1915, eventually making a three-day march from the coast down to Ypres in Belgium. Here they soon discovered the realities of being at the Front – no sooner had they been given their very first twenty-four-hour rest period than an enemy artillery bombardment rained down.

Major F. Wright of the Swindon Fortress engineers, captured by one of his men as he watches embarkation.

Swindon engineers with Cyril Spencer Wilson (assistant manager of the GWR Works) mounted and in greatcoat, and a French officer in front.

The Swindonians spent the next few weeks executing general fieldwork at St Eloi, having to make a three-hour march each day from their billets. Here, they repaired trenches, laid cables and dug a tunnel to provide hidden access to the front line. It was during this time that the Swindon Company received its first casualties, and its first honour. Lance Corporal J. Kent and Sapper Nash were wounded by rifle fire, while Company Sergeant Major Rodda was awarded the French Medaille Militaire for a survey he conducted at Brigade headquarters. As the company continued repairing and building infrastructure behind the front lines, more honours were bestowed on Swindon engineers, particularly since much of their work was done within the range of enemy shellfire; for example, Sergeant O. Davis and Sapper F. Perry both received Distinguished Conduct Medals for making instant repairs to a vital bridge over the canal at Yser, after a direct hit by enemy artillery. The constant rain of shells also called for the Swindon men to have considerable patience. Shortly after building huts for the 1st Cavalry Division at Yser, the engineers could do nothing but watch as enemy artillery reduced their hard work to little more than splinters.

The next few months saw the Swindon sappers engaged in what they described as 'the humdrum life of mechanics', creating

materials and equipment for the front-line troops, such as lighting for tunnel diggers at Messines, reinforced concrete machine-gun nests on Kemmel Hill, and the repair of a bridge at Houplines. During this time, Swindon engineers utilised the skills they brought from both the GWR Works and the Wiltshire agricultural industry, creating a wood mill at Bailleul powered completely by steam and receiving high praise from an inspector from the War Council.

In August, everything changed, with the unit being sent further south to the Somme where they were needed to lay pipes for supplying water to the soldiers in the trenches and the all-important horses. Two 4in pipelines were laid near Montauban-de-Picardie in flooded, mud-filled conditions that were so appalling that any horse that stepped off course was instantly trapped and had to be shot. Then the rain turned to ice. From November 1916 until March 1917, the men worked through a winter where the temperature sometimes fell as low as -15½°C, and the local river froze over completely. Throughout, the engineers had to keep water flowing, creating a water pumping station at Maricourt that was driven by three sets of 70hp petrol engines, plus four sets of 40hp engines, all the while under the ever-present danger of shellfire. With patrols and repair detachments out all day and all night, the Swindon engineers maintained the pipes despite them being laid under 2½ft of frozen mud and constantly being damaged by frost or artillery. Nonetheless, by the end of winter the men took pride in the fact that theirs was the only system in the area that had not failed, despite the extreme conditions.

One Step Forward

From February 1917, the Swindon Fortress engineers moved from one place to another depending on the unpredictable give-and-take of trench warfare. As the Germans were pushed back to what the Allies referred to as the 'Hindenburg Line' the company moved to Foucaucourt to construct a corps headquarters. They built another at Villers-Carbonnel, for the Fourth Army, and, over the following months, constructed casualty clearing stations, huts, water supplies, bridges and, at one point, even a railway platform designed for loading wounded men onto ambulance trains which, in all probability, had been built in Swindon. The unit also spent some four months at Dunkirk, under constant night-time attack from German aeroplanes.

As the Allied troops thrust forward at Cambrai in November 1917, the engineers were once again called up to the front, primarily to fill in craters on the Bapaume–Cambrai road, exposed to enemy machine-gun fire as well as suffering from hunger due to a severe lack of rations. When the men initially arrived at the road, they had no idea where the enemy was placed and all climbed down from their motor lorries in sight of the German line. Although some of the men were wounded in the action that followed, most managed to defend themselves, digging in and using hedges to hide their position. Following a night under canvas, one group of sergeants woke up to see Germans walking around in full view of their tent. A hasty dash to safer quarters was just in time, as the tent received a direct hit seconds later. Things did not get much better for a while. When food finally arrived and was set up to be prepared, the site received a direct artillery hit and the food was ruined. But that was not going to stop Swindonian Quartermaster Sergeant Duck, who

Some of the sites where Swindon engineers saw service along the Western Front.

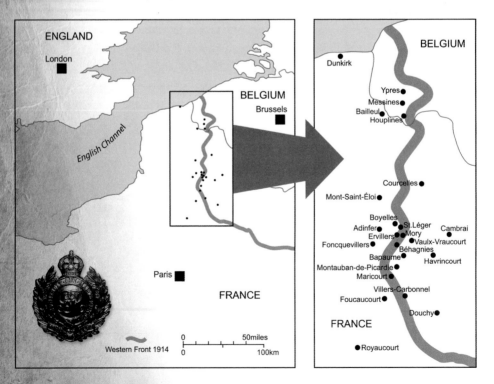

prepared another lot, single-handed, and helped to deliver it to the hungry men even as they were responding to the attack. Duck was awarded the Distinguished Conduct Medal for his bravery.

Despite the slightly inauspicious start, a detachment of the engineers later set about the creation of the 'Yellow Line', at Vaulx-Vraucourt, comprising machine-gun emplacements, new trenches and barbed wire entanglements, which initially held up 'wave after wave' of German infantry.

However, just as the Swindon engineers moved forwards whenever the army itself made progress, the reverse was also true. As the German Spring Offensive kicked off in March 1918, the unit was moved further and further back, digging, then abandoning trenches, or on occasion not even getting as far as digging due to the speed of the German onslaught. Finally, the company managed to settle for a while, after suffering aerial bombardments, total lack of sleep, and a not very pleasant stay in a barn where they had to come to 'an amicable understanding with a squad of pigs who were already in possession'. On arrival at the Adinfer-Foncquevillers area, a firm line of trenches was established, and the engineers had the pride of seeing a trench named 'The Swindon Trench' with a bridge they constructed over it which was so like one back home near the Golden Lion pub, they named it 'Golden Lion' Bridge.

After 21 August 1918, the Swindon engineers were again moving forward. One of their recurring tasks was the establishing of water points and at Douchy theirs was the only one to survive heavy artillery fire. As a consequence, the place rapidly filled with thousands of horses, including those of the Royal Field Artillery, causing one engineer to note: 'The country was black with them; I didn't think there was so many horses in the world.' From here, the company moved forward to work at Courcelles, Ervillers, St Leger, Mory, Behagnies, and Vaulx-Vraucourt, supporting the Allied advances.

Heavy Engineering

The latter days of the war did not reduce the workload, nor the risks for Swindon's engineering company. In the construction of a massive ramp at Royaucourt, some 300ft long and 10ft wide, a working party was caught by a German barrage and suffered such losses that

*Swindon and New
Zealand men in
front of the largest
military bridge in
France, which they
created over the
Canal du Nord.*

*Ramp at
Royaucourt, built by
Swindon engineers.*

the company had to be sent back to Boyelles for recovery. Even then the work didn't stop, and the men were joined by New Zealand engineers to build a massive steel bridge across the Canal du Nord, near Havrincourt. The bridge spanned 180ft, with an overall length of 240ft and a launching weight of 120 tons, making it the largest military bridge in the country and causing Sir Douglas Haig himself to inspect it at least twice during construction. As the Allied forces pushed on, the engineers kept up with them, building and repairing bridges as they went, right up to the day of the Armistice. Tragically, the day before peace was announced, a party of six Swindon men was working on a bridge when a German mine went off, killing them all.

Even after the Armistice, there was still work for the Swindon engineers in the long and arduous dismantling of the war machine and rebuilding of basic infrastructure. The Swindon Company of the Wiltshire (Fortress) Royal Engineers was finally ordered to stand down on 19 November 1919, over a year after the war had ended.

Send in the Cavalry: 'D' Squadron, Royal Wiltshire Yeomanry

The Prince of Wales' Own Royal Regiment of Yeomanry was, at the outset of the war, the oldest such regiment in the country, having been formed in 1779. Swindon was extremely proud to have its own

Men of the Swindon Yeomanry setting off to camp.

squadron of the yeomanry: 'D' Squadron, Royal Wiltshire Yeomanry. But the cavalry skills that had served the yeomen well for 150 years needed updating in the arts of war specific to the new circumstances. Part of their training was to cross rivers with 150 men, 170 horses, 2 machine guns and of course all the ammunition and kit. Apparently the Swindon men relished this sort of challenge, but unfortunately most of the training was not quite such fun. After months of 'mud and monotony', the Swindon squadron was finally attached to the 38th Division as Divisional Cavalry in September 1915, and readied for overseas service. By 5 December the men were in France, moving in rain and snow to Enguinegatte in the Hazebrouck district and their first taste of life on the front line. Of course, being cavalry, many of their duties were roles in despatch riding, road reconnaissance and keeping traffic in order. However, the men did also have to learn basic skills in wiring and trench making.

Some of the sites where the Yeomanry saw service along the Western Front, including Heudicourt, site of their last cavalry charge.

In the summer of 1916 the squadron moved to the Somme where they joined two squadrons of the South Irish Horse and were put on standby to follow up after initial artillery barrages and infantry charges. The battle did not go the way the Allied Forces hoped, and in

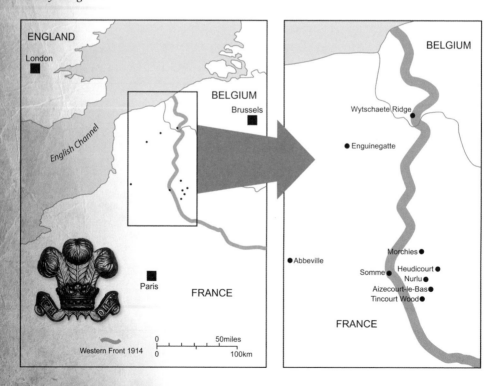

ENGLAND
London

English Channel

BELGIUM
Brussels

Paris
FRANCE

Western Front 1914

0   50miles
0   100km

BELGIUM

Wytschaete Ridge

● Enguinegatte

● Abbeville

Morchies ●
Somme ● ● Heudicourt ●
Nurlu ●
Aizecourt-le-Bas ●
Tincourt Wood ●

FRANCE

Company Sergeant Major Arthur Loveday, from Stafford Street, was hit by a German bullet in France but it was miraculously stopped by his own bullets. Sadly Arthur was later killed in action in 1918.

the end the Yeomanry were not called on in their cavalry capacity. Even so, the squadron was still on the front line and, through its observation role, suffered a number of casualties, including troop leader, Lieutenant Simmonds. During the same action Trooper Griffin was awarded the Military Cross for conspicuous daring.

The squadron was finally sent to a rest area at Abbeville in November 1916 where they rejoined with the other Wilts squadrons, meaning the Royal Wiltshire Yeomanry regiment was all together at the same time – a whole 'corps' of cavalry. Perhaps on account of them now being the cohesive whole that they were always intended to be, the winter of 1917 saw the Yeomanry take on much more of a 'traditional' cavalry role. Throughout a particularly fierce winter of snow and blizzards, the men and horses headed into occupied territory, sometimes 20 miles in advance of their infantry. Fighting as an independent unit, the men proactively sought out the enemy: on one patrol at Nurlu, they discovered a large force of motor machine guns and cyclists, and gave them a taste of the devastation a cavalry unit can wreak, forcing the enemy to evacuate the area. However, the overall conditions were not good. Being away from their own lines meant the men and their horses were exposed to the bitter winter weather with no shelter and, despite the devotion of the men, many horses sadly succumbed to the cold. Nonetheless, the Yeomanry moved further east and captured Aizecourt-le-Bas, then south to Tincourt Wood, and back up to Heudicourt, where they performed their last gallant cavalry charge, brandishing swords against an enemy of machine guns, artillery and rifle fire (see 106). Following their 'dismounting' in July 1917, the men of the proud Yeomanry were merged with the 6th Wiltshire Battalion and, in March 1918, were caught in a disastrous battle at Morchies, losing nearly all their men. The few remaining members of the Yeomanry moved into a 'mixed' battalion to see further action at Wytschaete Ridge in April 1918 and then finally into the 2nd Wiltshire Battalion.

CHARGE OF THE SWINDON BRIGADE

On 27 January 1885, the War Office sent a letter to Lord Bath saying: 'The Secretary of State has now submitted to Her Majesty a Precedence Table of Yeomanry Cavalry Regiments, and the position allotted to the Wiltshire Yeomanry Cavalry is No. 1.' For Swindon, this was a matter of some pride given that, at the outbreak of war, the town had its very own unit: 'D' Squadron, Royal Wiltshire Yeomanry. Unfortunately for the 120 Swindon yeomen, the squadron was almost instantly disbanded, with the men being split over the other three squadrons of the Wilts Yeomanry. Nonetheless, when volunteers for active service were called for, nearly all the members of 'D' Squadron stepped forward, and were promptly reformed into their original outfit.

The squadron served in various sectors of France, achieving a number of successful actions. However, in March 1917 they were to learn the limitations of horseback warfare in the new, 'modern' war. At Heudicourt, south-west of Cambrai, the Allies faced what they believed was three machine guns hiding in the local wood, as well as artillery and rifle fire. It was decided to give the task of clearing the area to 'D' Squadron, which took the role with pride, charging across three-quarters of a mile of open ground brandishing their swords. Sadly, the rain of machine-gun fire was devastating, and even before they had got a few hundred yards the charge was over, and the Yeomanry withdrew. Although the unit suffered five deaths and many wounded, it was the horses which took the main brunt, suffering very heavy losses.

In July 1917, to 'their deep disgust' the cavalrymen of the country's premier Yeomanry Regiment, were ordered that they should be dismounted. Following the sad delivery of their horses to Boulogne, the men marched to Rouen for infantry training, before being drafted into the 6th Wiltshire Battalion.

Members of the Yeomanry in more peaceful times, at a training camp in 1912.

Wiltshire Yeoman Frederick Hilton was taken prisoner on the same day his brother, Edgar, who was also a Yeoman, was killed in action.

Big Guns in India:
1st Battery (Wilts) Royal Field Artillery

Swindonians did not only serve at the Western Front. In 1914 the 3rd Wessex Brigade, Royal Field Artillery was composed of the 1st, 2nd and 3rd batteries, being known respectively as the Wilts, Hants and Dorset batteries, with the 1st Battery (Wilts) Royal Field Artillery being composed primarily of men from Swindon and its immediate surroundings. At that time a Royal Field Artillery Battery would usually comprise around 200 men. Not long after the war started, a second unit of the 1st Battery was formed, with the two units known as the First/First and First/Second, or 1/1 and 1/2.

The Swindon gunners were among the very first troops mobilised in August 1914, but their initial destination was not the Western Front. One of the consequences of so many men fighting in France and Belgium was that Britain's military commitments in other parts of the world became extremely stretched. As a result many territorial units were sent to far off places to free up regular troops for the main battlefronts. This was the case for both batteries of Swindon's 1st, with them both being posted to India, the 1/1 spending three years in Bombay, while the 2/1 spent the first two years in Trimulgherry. However there was no fighting in India, meaning the troops spent their time engaged in extremely rigorous artillery

Horses were essential for all areas of the war – these belong to the Royal Field Artillery. The rider is Swindonian Edgar Nicholas, killed in action in 1917.

Royal Field Artillery crew with an 18-pounder.

training, and, apparently, equally rigorous sporting efforts, winning prizes in hockey, horsemanship, football and cricket. But although the units stayed in India, the men themselves changed, with those whose training had progressed enough being sent off to war fronts while new recruits arrived from England to take their places. Men from both batteries found themselves fighting in France and Mesopotamia (an area covering modern-day Iraq, north-east Syria, and parts of Turkey, Iran and Kuwait). Even for those in India, there were still dangers. Unrest on India's border with Afghanistan (before the creation of Pakistan), meant 1/1 Battery was sent into potentially hostile country, settling at a border station between Rawalpindi and Nowshera. Although the gunners readied themselves behind the infantry and cavalry front, they were never called on to fire in anger. There were other dangers too. After a move down to Lahore, the men met an outbreak of cholera and discovered why the city was known as the 'White Man's Grave'. Three months holed up in the garrison led to an unknown number of casualties, including at least five men from Swindon: Battalion Sergeant Major H. George; Dr Leonard; Dr Pearce; Gunner Mills, and Bombardier Rand.

In April 1918, the last thirty-six men of the original 1/1 Battery were sent to France, while about fifteen men returned to England, and the battery effectively closed down. The men of 1/2 Battery, plus another later-formed 1/3 Battery moved around India, to places including Bangalore, Rajankunte, Meerut, Delhi, and even Afghanistan. They stayed in India until well after the end of the war, only landing in Liverpool in November 1919, after exactly five years of duty in the defence of the Empire.

The Highest Honour

Not all of Swindon's gunners ended up in India. Early in 1916 a brand new 'B' Battery was formed on Salisbury Plain, with men from Swindon, Dorset and Hampshire. Soon they found themselves in France where they met other men from Swindon who had been there since the start of the previous year. The battery was in action almost instantly, and having to cope with return artillery fire, gas attacks, and mines exploding nearby. On 13 August the battery was bombarded so severely – for twelve hours by 8in shells – that the king himself, who had been observing from Mont-Saint-Éloi, came the next day to see how they were, believing that they must all surely be dead. Miraculously, the battery was still more or less in one piece.

William Gosling wearing the Victoria Cross he earned on 5 April 1917 for leaving his trench to disarm a mortar round.

One draft of the 3rd Wessex Battery found its way to France with the 51st Highland Division, keeping together and serving throughout the war. The most notable figure in that unit for Swindonians was Wanborough man, Sergeant William Gosling, who was attached to a trench mortar battery. On 5 April 1917, Gosling left the trench to disarm a mortar round that had fallen only a few yards from his unit and a host of infantry. Gosling lifted the nose of the bomb up, unscrewed the fuse and hurled it into no-man's-land where it immediately exploded. Gosling's action saved a considerable number of lives and, for this act of valour, he was awarded the highest honour: the Victoria Cross. After the war, Gosling set up a dairy in Wroughton with an image of his Victoria Cross on all the bottles.

And Elsewhere

Following its action in northern France, 'B' Battery headed down to Marseilles and then, on 10 December 1917, on to the city of Salonika, in Greece. Following six months of action in the area, the battery was moved on again, this time to Egypt, but only for long enough to be re-equipped before making the long and arduous journey to the Be'er Sheba front, where they were instantly sent into action against the Turkish army in the Allies' Southern Palestine Offensive.

Despite a severe lack of water, the battery moved towards the city of Be'er Sheba and battled with the Turkish rearguard, pushing on to the river of Wadi Sharia just a few miles south of Gaza, near places the Allies named Charing Cross and Dorset Hill. Here the gunners became trapped in front of a 300ft-deep ravine on the Wadi Sharia, where the Turks had dug themselves in. Holding on for reinforcements, the battery was under machine gun and artillery bombardment for some nine hours, with twenty-three casualties and the loss of half its horses. After more heavy bombardment, and with determined fighting from the Allied side, the day was eventually won, and the battery was freed from its trapped position. The day got even better when Bombardier Baker turned up with cigarettes, which had been in seriously short supply!

On 9 December 1917, 'B' Battery of 3rd Wiltshire Brigade Royal Field Artillery, with its Swindon gunners, was the very first Allied unit to enter Jerusalem.

The areas of Salonika and Palestine where Swindon gunners saw action (shown with modern boundaries).

The advance continued, and 'B' Battery kept up its fire on the retreating enemy while on the move, heading northwards towards Gaza, and back to Sharia to be re-equipped for the final advance on Jerusalem. After firing on Turks along the Nablus road, the battery moved with the rest of the Allies into the city itself. Although the Turks had apparently surrendered, it was clear that they did not all know that, and 'B' Battery still had to do some fighting. Reports from the time describe how overwhelmed with relief the inhabitants were in their welcoming of the Allies. Life had clearly been very tough under Turkish occupation. In particular, the residents had suffered from the Turks taking whatever they wanted, without payment or consideration of the hardships caused. The inhabitants soon realised this would not be the case with the 'courteous' newcomers, and the price of everything suddenly rose rather dramatically. But the battle was not over. The Turks were not going to let Jerusalem go that easily, and 'B' Battery spent the whole of the first night, and much of the following week, still engaged with enemy fire.

The next six months were spent moving from place to place as required, almost constantly in action, even when supposedly at rest. Finally, the battery marched over 30 miles by night, to just north of Jaffa, to be part of General Allenby's finishing blow against the Turks on 19 September 1918. The battery joined a formidable line of 18-pounders, four-point-fives, 6in guns, 8in guns, and even naval guns, to pound the enemy into total submission.

7

MOONRAKERS ACROSS THE WORLD

In the early years of the twentieth century, Swindon's influence spread across the world, through the export of its railway knowledge, hardware, technology and skills. In the Great War, the town's men also spread out across the globe. In fact, there is a Swindon connection to almost every military service, all the different theatres of war, and every major event. As well as populating the four Swindon-based units mentioned in the previous chapter, many Swindon men also joined their county's regiment, the Wiltshire Regiment, particularly as Kitchener created ever-more battalions in response to international needs. Beyond that, Swindon men also served on the seas and in the air, in tanks and submarines, and in every other field available.

The Wiltshires

The infantry units of the Wiltshire Regiment (Duke of Edinburgh's) were formed officially in 1881 after the regiment's predecessor, the 62nd (Wiltshire) Regiment of Foot, formed in 1756, was joined by the 99th Duke of Edinburgh's (Lanarkshire) Regiment of Foot. One of the regiment's nicknames was 'The Moonrakers', after a Wiltshire tale of smugglers fooling customs officers. The tale goes that the locals had hidden barrels of illegal contraband on a riverbed and, while recovering them at night, they were disturbed by the officers. With a bit of quick thinking, the men pointed at the reflection of the moon on the

The stiffened service dress cap worn by most soldiers during the Great War, with the badge of the Wiltshire Regiment.

water and claimed they were trying to rescue a large round cheese. This meant that outsiders were led to believe Wiltshiremen were very stupid, while the Wiltshiremen knew they had outsmarted the officers and were free to carry on just as they pleased. Whatever anyone else thought of the Wiltshires before the war, they soon found out that they were a force to be reckoned with.

The regiment was in the thick of the fighting from the very start of the war, suffering casualties and gaining honours throughout the four years, in all the major battle arenas. The regiment's role is impossible to encapsulate here, but the words of King George V in 1915 express something of how they were viewed by the rest of the world, even in the earlier days: 'The Wiltshire Regiment has done splendidly in this war. In fact, I can say that no regiment has done better.' The regiment's name was even well known by the enemy. On one occasion, a group of men approached the Wilts' trenches in what looked suspiciously like Wilts' uniforms. As Bavin reports of the incident, the men were shouting: '"Nein, nein! Leedle mistake. Ve are de Vilts." The dialect was hardly suggestive of the Downs, and the English officer gave the order to charge.' Admittedly, anyone listening to the marching song of the Wiltshire Regiment might have found themselves wondering just what language the Wiltshiremen were using. The song, about flies on turnips, has a chorus which goes: 'The vly, the vly. The vly be on the turmut, 'Tis all me eye, For Oi to try, To keep vlies off them turmuts.'

Swindon Terriers

For Swindon, there was a particularly strong connection to the 4th Wiltshire Battalion (the Duke of Edinburgh's Wiltshire Regiment of Territorials) which in 1914 already included 152 Swindon 'Terriers', making up 'H' Company, or the Swindon

Company. In August 1914, the whole of 4th Wilts Battalion (a battalion could be up to 800 men) was at Bulford Camp engaged in its annual training like many other units connected to Swindon.

By 9 October, the Swindon men were on their way to India with some of their townsfolk in the batteries of the 3rd Wessex Brigade, Royal Field Artillery. Following the creation of an additional battalion, the 2/4, the original battalion was designated the First/Fourth (1/4). No sooner had the 1/4 gone, than the 2/4 was following in its wake, also bound for India but on a slightly more eventful journey. Their ship, the *Saturnia*, caused most men to suffer seasickness and crashed near Gibraltar into a wooden, three-masted schooner which came off considerably worse in the encounter. After restocking with coal at Port Said, according to Bavin, the men spent the rest of the voyage with coal dust permeating everything, including clothes, belongings, beds, and even their food.

The 2/4 was destined to spend the whole of the war in India, but for their Swindon comrades in 'H' Company of the 1/4, India was only the first part of their story. The company's early duties included the defence of the Fort of Delhi, where the entire European population of the Indian capital resided in case of local uprising. Life was relatively quiet here, with the men enjoying local festivities and hospitality, as well as tobacco, letters and other luxuries sent from home, including Christmas parcels paid for by the efforts of the Empire Theatre in Swindon. However, although it was described as 'a home from home', regular drafts were sent off to other fronts

2/4 Battalion after a parade in India.

Wiltshiremen showing off their hyena 'trophy' after hunting near Delhi.

as needs arose. The first such draft headed to Mesopotamia in May 1915, with others following soon after. By September nearly all the original men were in Mesopotamia, in what is now Iraq. By November, near Baghdad, one draft of the battalion suffered such losses that it was nearly wiped out altogether.

The core 1/4 Battalion remained in Delhi for another two years, with summer visits to hill stations as a break from the heat, before making preparations for active service itself. On 15 September 1917 the men set sail from Bombay bound for Egypt, and then on to Palestine where they were to be part of General Allenby's force.

The Swindon Company was in action within a fortnight, at Gaza, and one of the first casualties was Private J.H. Woodham. The company's commanding officer was Captain T.N. Arkell, of the well-known brewery family back home. Arkell wrote at the time:

> It is with the deepest regret that I sit down to write and tell you about the death of your son, Private J.H. Woodham, who was killed this morning. A raid on the Turks had just taken place (which was a great success), and they in return started to shell our trenches heavily at about 4 a.m. Your son was in a trench with three other men carrying out his duty by standing-to with his rifle grenades, when an unlucky shell landed in the middle of the trench and exploded.

117

In November 1917, the 1/4 Wilts were part of the force that took Jerusalem. Shortly after the taking of the city, Captain Arkell himself was wounded by rifle fire at a small outpost on a nearby hill-position. As the winter went on, and the 'rainy season' settled in, the unit moved north of Jerusalem, to collect and process captured enemy ammunition, including 77,740 small arms cartridges, belts of 96,600 machine-gun cartridges and over 2,000 bombs of various types.

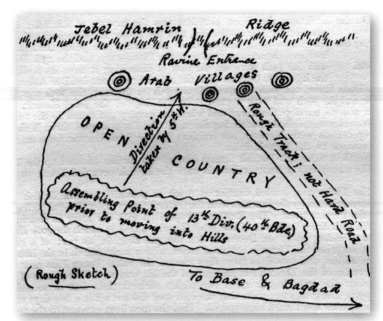

Hand-drawn diagram by a Swindon private in Mesopotamia.

Wiltshires among the pyramids. Many of the battalions went to Egypt, some to fight and some in transit to Palestine and Mesopotamia.

Spring 1918 saw the Allies renew efforts against the Turks, moving slightly further north to Rafat where the 1/4 was heavily involved in an unsuccessful battle which cost the Wiltshires a large number of casualties. The men spent the next six weeks dug in around two hills they called 'Tin Hat Hill' and 'Toogood Hill'. Eventually things calmed down as the Allied Forces achieved domination over the Turks in the area and the 1/4 moved to the orange groves of the Vale of Sharon to take part in the British advance that started on 19 September. Despite the loss of more men, including their leader, Colonel A. Armstrong, the 1/4th Wilts Battalion took several trench lines and covered some 5 miles, supported by heavy artillery fire.

The Other Wiltshires

Although 4th Battalion was particularly important in Swindon's part in the war, many men from the town and surrounding area ended up in other battalions of their county's regiment, the Wiltshire Regiment, and there were a lot of them: two original regular battalions (1st and 2nd), then 3rd Battalion as a special reserve unit; 4th Battalion with its two 'versions', 1/4 and 2/4; then four 'service' battalions created because of the war (5th, 6th, 7th and 8th). It is impossible to describe the activity of the whole regiment here, but given the involvement of Swindonians, it is appropriate to at least give a few snippets.

Group of men of the 7th Battalion, Wiltshire Regiment before they headed off to France and then Salonika

Right from the Start

On 18 August 1914, the 1st Wiltshire Battalion landed at Le Havre as part of the First Expeditionary Force. Within a few days, the battalion was bombarded by German artillery, even before they had time to dig trenches. As the Germans pushed relentlessly towards Paris, the regiment fought in the Allied line in the decisive Battle of Marne, halting the German advance, and pushing them back to the River Aisne. The observations of a trooper in the 2nd Dragoon Guards who was there describes the Wiltshires:

> On our left at the Battle of Aisne were the Wiltshires, located in trenches just outside a wood. The Germans came through the wood in mass, and when at the edge charged the Wiltshires with bugles blowing and yelling like demons. We watched breathlessly, but the boys knew what they were doing. At about seventy-five yards range an officer sprang from the trench and yelled 'Fire!' Then the Germans got a taste of Hell in the form of 15 rounds a minute. They wavered like drunken men. The Wiltshires then sprang from the trenches and charged with the bayonet. It was awful suspense while they rushed, and then came the impact. It was a horrible din, but at the finish what remained of the Germans fled back through the wood, and as the dusk settled down all that could be heard were the groans of the wounded.

Clearly the Wiltshires were professional soldiers. Indeed, the 1st was one of the regular battalions, and following their success at Marne, the men moved on to Ypres where they were joined by their comrades in the other regular Wilts battalion, the 2nd. As Christmas approached, bad weather kept the Wiltshiremen in trenches which were full of mud and water, occasionally up to the waist, with the men unable to ever dry out and, most of the time, unable to even sit down. In some areas of Kemmel the water was so deep that the only way to defend the trenches was with men bobbing about in barrels. Despite, or perhaps because of these terrible conditions, Christmas Day and Boxing Day saw an informal truce between the Wiltshires and their German counterparts, with the two sides burying their dead comrades and holding occasional conversations.

As the troops would have been painfully aware, the war was not 'over by Christmas'. With the two Wilts battalions reinforced by men from 'Kitchener's Army', the Wiltshiremen fought in the Battle of Neuve Chapelle, the second Battle of Ypres in April, and, in May and June 1915, adding Festubert and Hooge to their battle list. In July, their comrades in the 5th battalion landed in Gallipoli where, in early August, their brave stand contributed to their division becoming known as the 'Iron Division' in the *Egyptian Gazette* newspaper.

In September 1915, the 1st and 2nd Wilts went into another major battle at Loos, along with the 6th Wilts, which had only recently arrived in France but already been bloodied at Laventie and Festubert. On Thursday, 23 September, the 2nd Wilts marched in pouring rain to a village 5 miles behind the lines before making their way up to the front at 9 p.m. on the Friday before the battle. It proved to be a terrible occasion, with British and Allied men going 'over the top' to face withering fire from artillery, rifles and well-embedded machine guns, after a poor artillery barrage and an early attempt to use gas both failed to sufficiently soften up the enemy. The Swindon press at the time gives a hint of the divide between the world of the soldier and

Swindon gunner Albert Slade (left) was a proficient horse rider, but here he swaps his horse for a camel in Egypt.

the folk back home. On the day of the battle, the small ads in the *Swindon Advertiser* offered billiards tables, bicycles and other bargains, while the only coverage the battle got was a couple of days later, in a very short communiqué from Sir John French:

> British Capture Loos. Between La Bassee and Lens the British have advanced at some points two and a half miles on a front five miles long, capturing Loos and a hill within a half of Lens and taking nearly 2,000 prisoners.

After the battle, the commander of the 1st Wilts observed that a number of lessons should be learned. For example, he noted that trenches dug the night before an advance, despite not being of a very high standard, survived well on account of the enemy not having time to record them; telephone cables laid over-ground were useless, because enemy artillery destroyed them; and many unnecessary casualties were caused by orderlies not being sure of the position of Battalion Headquarters.

Hardships and Victories

In March 1916, the 5th Wilts joined the Mesopotamian Expeditionary Forces in a campaign against the Turks, in modern-day Iraq. In thunderstorms, hailstorms and hurricanes that turned the place into a quagmire, clogged up guns and flooded trenches, the Wiltshiremen fought against the ever-resilient Turks. Then, in summer, the temperature rose to 50°C and the men had to contend with terrible sickness, including cholera, dysentery, boils and jaundice. Similar conditions were suffered by the men of the 7th, facing the Bulgarian Army in Macedonia, with malaria killing thousands of men. Local men's deaths were reported back home in the casualty lists of the *Swindon Advertiser* and the *North Wilts Herald*.

The 1st moved in June to the Somme front, ready for the 'Big Push' of 1916. The fighting there continued through July and in August led to the 1st Wilts facing the 'legendary' Prussian Guard at Thiepval.

The Mark V tank could reach speeds of almost 5 miles per hour, had a radius of action of 25 miles, and could turn even when climbing a slope. It had a 150hp six-cylinder, poppet-valve Ricardo engine with epicyclic gears, a turret, and Hotchkiss machine guns.

As described by Australian newspaper, *The Argus*: 'The men of the corps are the supposed super troops of the Kaiser's army, hallowed by legend with unconquerable prowess. Their officers are exclusively noble and the rank and file must be at least 5ft 10in and 12st.' None of that put off the Wiltshiremen. On 24 July, they, along with the Worcesters, went over the top and with bombs, machine guns and hand-to-hand fighting, eventually defeated the 93rd regiment of the Prussian Guard Fusiliers. The war diary for the 27th was typically military: 'Baths were allotted to the Battalion at Hedauville and Acheux. There were foot inspections in the afternoon.'

Photograph of a Prussian soldier as a memento for a Swindon man.

From the end of 1916 up to April 1917, the 7th Wilts was entrenched against the Bulgarian army on the Greek/Macedonian border, but military and political secrecy meant that very little of their action was reported back home, leading to some thinking that the opposing armies were simply sitting there staring at each other. In truth, on 24 April 1917, the battalion was practically wiped out at Doiran by machine-gun fire, losing nearly all its officers and some 300 other men. George James Smith, from Rodbourne, was one of ten Swindon men who vanished without trace that night. Tragically, or perhaps fittingly, part of the battle area was known by the Allied troops as Swindon Hill.

In France the 6th suffered similar scale losses at Passchendaele between September and November 1917, with one Swindon casualty, Captain H.H. Williams, being mentioned twice in despatches by Field Marshall Sir Douglas Haig. Williams was commander of 'C' Company and before the war had been a teacher under the Swindon Education Committee, a profession in which he excelled as much as he did in the army. He was 23 when he died.

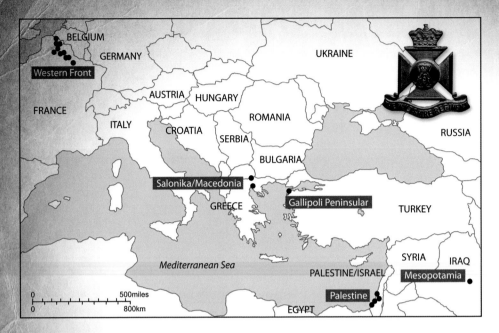

The main areas
of engagement
for the Wiltshires
(shown with
modern boundaries).

Towards the end of 1917, the 6th was joined by more Swindonians when the Royal Wilts Yeomanry was merged with the battalion. At the Battle of Cambrai, on 20 November, 330 tanks led an advance to Anneux, with many of the tank drivers having been trained by Swindonian William George Blake (*see* Chapter 2: Preparations at Home). But there was a price. The Tank Corps suffered some 600 casualties, and, in the huge number of casualties of the supporting infantry, Swindon lost two members of home football teams: Frederick Wheatcroft, centre forward for Swindon Town, and Reginald Menham, goalkeeper for Swindon Corinthians and reserve goalkeeper for Swindon Town.

Tide Turning

March–July 1918 was to prove a decisive time in the Great War, with the Germans launching the massive Spring Offensive. The Wiltshires were inevitably in the thick of things, with the 2nd Wilts facing the whole weight of the German onslaught at St Quentin in March, including an obliterating artillery barrage and 'countless' waves of infantry. The battalion suffered over

600 casualties. On that same evening, the 6th were digging in at Beugny/Morchies, thinking they were 2 miles behind the front. Unfortunately, the Germans were advancing at such a rate that very soon the Wiltshires were under bombardment. By 6 p.m. on Monday, 23 March, the Allied line was broken and the Wiltshiremen were surrounded. Only about thirty men made it safely back to their lines.

In August the tide finally turned, with the Allies launching a counter-operation starting with the Battle of Amiens on 8 August, a day that was called 'the black day of the German Army' by German General Erich Ludendorff. A number of Swindon men were involved in Amiens. One in particular, Sid Philips, was a friend of tank trainer William Blake, and suffered the terrible fate of being burned to death in his tank. Philips has no known grave, but is remembered on a memorial at Vis en Artois, alongside other Swindon fallen: Walter Gee, Frederick Arthur Balch, and Bennett Newman. Throughout the rest of the war Wiltshiremen were in constant action as the Allies advanced across Europe. At the end of it all, the 1st Wilts found itself within 10 miles of where it had started over four years earlier.

Albert Fluck, father of Swindonian screen legend Diana Dors, served with the Wiltshires at Fort Delhi in India. In 1917 he was sent to Egypt, then Palestine, and finally France where he almost lost an eye on the Western Front.

More than Khaki

Although most Swindon men ended up in the army, with many of them joining the Wiltshires, they were also represented in other forces. The navy in particular was very popular with many people in Swindon and the town had its own reservists. Consequently, a number of Swindonians found themselves on board ship, often in roles connected with the heavy engineering aspects of the huge ships of the time. Of course, this also meant that Swindon men lost their lives at sea during the war, such as F. Beard, a 33-year-old labourer from the Works and a Naval reservist. Beard lost his life on HMS *Good Hope* on 1 November 1914 at the Battle of Coronel, off the coast of Chile. Swindonian William Luke Saloway (17) and fellow

HMS Vanguard *exploded at Scapa Flow on 9 July 1917, killing over 800 men.*

townsman Arthur Marshall were on HMS *Hampshire* at the Battle of Jutland when it went down with Lord Kitchener also on board in June 1916, off the coast of Orkney. Dennis Arthur Knee, a member of the Marine Artillery, was killed in what was called at the time the worst naval disaster in the history of the Royal Navy when his ship, HMS *Vanguard*, exploded at Scapa Flow on 9 July 1917, killing over 800 men.

Another member of a marines unit was Arthur Kemble, who served in the Dardanelles from October 1915. Kemble was evacuated from the SS River Clyde, and by 1 June 1916 was in France in the Lens/Vimy sector. In September he moved to the Somme where he was involved in an attack near Beaumont Hamel. Kemble was badly wounded when attempting to throw a German bomb back to the enemy. Eventually, after gangrene set in, he was evacuated back to Britain, or 'Blighty' as it was known, where he was discharged as a result of his wounds.

Swindon was also represented below the waves. Edward William Bevan was an engine-room artificer 3rd-Class submariner on board HMS *E16*. Bevan was one of those lost on 22 August 1916 when the submarine vanished with all hands after last being sighted 35 miles off Yarmouth. It was in all likelihood destroyed by depth charges from an enemy ship. Bevan's wife, Mable Hurst, and son and daughter had to move back to Swindon from Plymouth after he died, where they struggled to make ends meet.

Edward William Bevan, an engine-room artificer, was one of those lost when his submarine vanished off Yarmouth.

Highworth Warneford School takes its name from Lieutenant Rex Warneford, a pilot in the Royal Naval Air Service who was awarded the Victoria Cross for bringing down a Zeppelin over Brussels on 6 June 1915. The Warneford family owned a sixteenth-century manor house in nearby Sevenhampton.

Submarine of the type that Edward Bevan was on board.

Swindonians also played their part in the 'newest' of the services: Charles William Roberts, for example, was a sergeant in 34th Squadron Royal Flying Corps. Roberts is also an example of how far and wide Swindonians served – he was killed in action in Italy on 26 December 1917.

Swindon and the Empire

As part of the British Empire, it was inevitable that Swindon would build connections with other parts of the world, particularly given the influence of the railways in other countries where Britain had interests. As a consequence, Swindon men signed up with Canadian and South African regiments, and some eighty-two fought with the armies of Australia and New Zealand (ANZACs). Two such men, John and Charles Kirby, were the sons of J.P. Kirby, the man whose name appears on a multitude of birth, death and marriage certificates as he was a registrar in Swindon. The two brothers, previously pupils at Sanford Street School, emigrated to Australia in 1908 and both ended

Badge of the Australian and New Zealand troops (ANZACs).

up in Australian regiments, John as company sergeant major in 1st Battalion Australian Imperial Force (AIF), and Charles as a sergeant in 33rd Battalion AIF. Tragically, the brothers were both killed in the fighting. John died in Gallipoli on 2 May 1916, but has no known grave, while Charles died from bombing injuries sustained from using his body to protect another injured man. Another Antipodean connection was Private Thomas George Hunt who was born in New Zealand in 1886, but by 1891 was living in Coped Hall, Wootton Bassett, on the edge of Swindon. However, in 1911 he emigrated to Canada where he joined the Western Ontario Regiment (18th Battalion) and was killed in action on 11 November 1917 in Belgium. He is buried in the Passchendaele New British Cemetery.

8

Coming Home

Swindon spent 11 November 1918 celebrating, like most places in Britain. Despite drizzling rain, the streets filled with people – schoolchildren turned up at school only to be told to go again – ribbons, banners, flags, bands, and impromptu processions coloured everywhere, and the Works shut down for the afternoon. By evening, the town was awash with lights, all turned on in celebration of the restrictions being lifted, and the churches were filled with people giving thanks for the armistice, which was, as Bavin describes it, 'suspending the terrible slaughter which had been wringing the heart of humanity'. The thanks were not limited to church services – the Mayor of Swindon sent the following telegram to Field Marshal Sir Doulas Haig:

> On your victorious return home I desire on behalf of the inhabitants of Swindon respectfully to tender you our warmest thanks for the magnificent services you have rendered to the Empire in defeating and destroying Prussian militarism and so saving the liberties of all freedom-loving peoples. We tender our like appreciation and thanks to all the officers and men under your command. We beg also to assure you of our most heartfelt and lasting gratitude.

Events and activities began more formally on 'Mayor's Sunday', with a procession followed by a packed church service. As well as the national anthem, a number of hymns were sung, including 'Now thank we all our God', translated from the German hymn,

Children of King William Church of England School celebrating the peace in 1918.

Staff of Compton's, Swindon uniform makers, take a break to celebrate the end of the war.

'Nun danket alle Gott'. Originally written in 1636 by Lutheran, Martin Rinkart, the hymn had been a key thanksgiving tune for German festivals and also had something of a history of being sung after wars; it was sung in the seventeenth century when the Treaty of Westphalia was signed, and again after the Battle of Leuthen in 1757.

In the days that followed, the town did its best to settle back to everyday life and, for the most part, things carried on much as they had. Inevitably, there were reminders of the war, such as 'Victory Balls' – dances to honour various aspects of the war, with the great and the good usually in attendance. The finest of these in Swindon was reputedly the Municipal Victory Ball, hosted by the mayor and mayoress on 21 February 1919. With important guests including MP Sir Frederick Young, local landowners the Goddards and the Calleys, and a full house of other citizens, the event was a great success and included a collection for the Victoria Hospital and the Milton Road Nursing Home.

The 'Real' End of the War

Celebrations picked up again later in the year because, although the armistice was signed in November 1918, a full treaty was not finalised until 28 June 1919. A real sense of celebration again swept the town, but this time it was considerably more thoughtful, and generally less excitable. Sunday, 6 July was declared by royal proclamation to be 'Peace Sunday', and a sombre church service was held, preceded by a procession of soldiers of the 16th Worcester Regiment and a host of discharged and injured soldiers. Two weeks later, starting on Saturday, 19 July, a long weekend of activities took place, this time all properly organised in advance:

- The mayor and civic dignitaries invited all demobbed men to the town hall for the mayor to shake them by the hand, and offer them cigars and cigarettes.
- The mayor also extended an invitation for ex-servicemen to attend a special evening of entertainment being laid on at the Empire Theatre.
- During heavy rain, a sports event at the County Ground had a number of novelty races, to add to the entertainment. As well as relay races between local football clubs, there was a 'needle and thread' race, and a 'boat race', both of which apparently went down very well with the large crowd present.
- 4,300 children attended local theatres and picture houses for free with tickets that had been given out at schools the previous day.
- Free concerts were given in the town hall, where the borough's military band and a number of choirs joined local soloists to provide the musical entertainment.
- Dinners were laid on for older folk and widows of servicemen, many in their 80s or even 90s. Approximately 650 were fed at the drill hall and a further 200 enjoyed their meal at the corn exchange. Apparently, pipes and tobacco were provided for the men after the meals, and fruit and tea for the ladies.
- A memorial tree was planted in Town Gardens, in the pouring rain, near the Westlecot entrance.

- On Sunday, 20th July, another memorial service was held at the town hall. Hundreds of people made a procession to the service, while at the GWR Park over 10,000 people came together for an outdoor service.
- On Monday, 21st July, the event was replicated for children, with an estimated 11,000 children mustering in the park with flags, girls in coloured paper bonnets, and small children in decorated prams.

The thoughts underlying the events over the weekend can perhaps be encapsulated by a single phrase from the GWR park service: 'Let us remember before God the brave and the true who have died the death of Honour, and have departed into the Resurrection of Eternal Life, especially those men who from this town have fallen in the War.'

Dismantling the War Machine

It was the returning soldiers who provided the real evidence that hostilities were over. Just as the town's railway stations and Chiseldon Camp were so instrumental in the distribution of troops at the outset of the war, so they were for soldiers returning from France and beyond. The town was once again filled with columns of men, this time with their kit looking worse for wear, and often still covered in mud. Perhaps the other major difference was soldiers' attitudes. Regardless of how packed the trains were, or what other limits there were to food, drink and service, the troops were all in fantastically high spirits, clutching the rail warrants that would take them home again.

Many of the men who passed through Swindon would have already officially left, or be leaving, the army, having volunteered for 'the duration'. Those regulars who still had time to serve would of course have to fulfil that obligation. In all cases, the men were keen to get home as soon as possible, though they had to accept that the practicalities of dealing with such numbers did not make things easy for the co-ordinators. Furthermore, the military still had obligations across France and in other corners of the Empire, particularly since the armistice was simply a cessation of action,

Swindon marine Herbert Dunn's demobilisation certificate.

not the formal signing of a permanent treaty. In sending the men home, many of them without secure jobs to go to, the authorities also had to consider the very real threat of unrest and even revolution. As a consequence of these factors, the demobilisation process was long and slow through 1919, and in order of priority. Older and wounded men were obviously among those first released, with regulars who had served their time and early enlisters also arriving back before conscripted men.

Inevitably, Chiseldon Camp became a demobilisation centre and dispersal unit, and men soon started arriving, keen to return to their civilian lives. But the paperwork, paying of final wage packets, handing over of kit, and organisation of travel permits was all done in 'indescribable confusion' according to Lord Dunalley, who was appointed to take charge of the demobilisation at the camp. As more and more troops arrived from the port at Southampton, processes streamlined, with as many as 10,000 men being dealt with on days that started at 6 a.m. However, there were still issues, with one of the more serious incidents involving a minor revolution among the men who were doing the actual processing – they wanted to know when they too would be released and about 1,000 of them staged a protest. The impromptu revolution was quashed in a matter of seconds after Dunalley announced: 'There are Lewis guns in position commanding every street. My signal on the telephone and they open fire. Ten seconds to get to your huts.'

Curiously, Chiseldon was not where men of the Wiltshire Regiment were demobbed, and of course many Swindon men ended up in different regiments or services. As a result, local men turned up in their home town in dribs and drabs, as their units were gradually wound up in different parts of the country, or they were released from their duties elsewhere. Some Swindon men did not see their home town again until late in 1919, or even 1920. By then, Chiseldon Camp was starting the process of dismantling, with auctions in April and July to dispose of buildings (huts, dining halls, stables, etc.) as well as kitchen equipment and toilets. For a brief spell, Swindon Council considered the site as a potential solution to a housing shortage that was envisaged, but nothing ever came of the idea. Eventually, the buildings that were not sold off became the site of the School of Military Administration, and the demobbed men of Swindon started to settle back into life back home.

Flagging Support

With so many men returning home, there were inevitably concerns about the impact this would have on the town. The first signs that a return to normality was not going to be straightforward just because the war was officially over, came hot on the heels of the grand weekend of celebrations. As part of the celebrations, Swindon Council decided to erect a flagpole outside the town hall to fly a 'Peace Flag'. The pole reputedly cost the then-huge sum of £250, and was sited so that it would be prominent to those coming up from New Town. Unfortunately, not everyone thought this was appropriate and soon crowds of angry Swindonians, mostly ex-servicemen, began protesting around the town, and eventually burnt down the flagpole (*see* p.138). The riots continued sporadically for another few days, before the police turned out in force with truncheons ready. After an appeal from the chief constable, peace was gradually restored. Nonetheless, the mixture of happy and sad events to mark the end of the war, combined with the discontent visible in the riots, gives a good indication of the ambivalent feelings about things at that time.

Most enlisted men earned medals (these particular ones belonged to Swindon man, Gunner James Farrell), and were given cigars and certificates, but these could not feed their family.

Normal Life?

In many ways life did return to some sort of normality. Families got back together; husbands and wives re-established their commitments to each other; men went back to work where they could; children played, went to school and grew up; and the promenading of young folk, along the Marlborough Road for example, went back to being a world of young courting couples, after years of domination by groups of young, single women. And the same important issues were still there as ever: work, housing, heating and food. But the idea that life would simply go back to how it was before the war was sadly a long way from reality.

From a practical point of view, most post-war issues came down to the state of the economy: the colossal price rises that shortages had created and the corresponding general level of inflation.

Romance blossomed again after the war: George Snook and the new Mrs Edie Snook.

Nationally, the value of the pound had plummeted over the four years, down to something like 30 per cent of its pre-war value. This meant the government turned to the production of more paper money as it was cheaper to produce than metal. In 1919, it looked as though large numbers of five-shilling notes would be introduced, with the cost of silver rising so far that the five-shilling coin was in danger of costing more than its spending value to produce. As elsewhere, in Swindon this simply meant people were able to buy less with what they had. Following a question in parliament, it was revealed that in 1919, £1 was worth between 30 and 40*d* if you tried buying a pair of boots; for men's suits, between 35 and 40*d*; cotton goods, between 25 and 35*d*; and wool underwear, between 25 and 30*d*.

As if the value of money was not bad enough, the shortage of commodities continued, and the price of goods continued to rise initially. With the war over, the needs of 'enemy' countries now became part of the same global economy as Britain, with all parties competing for the same resources. At home, Swindon's Food Control Committee had a few attempts to lift cost-controls and rations on certain products, only to find that prices instantly rocketed, putting them even further out of the reach of everyday folk. Consequently, strict controls remained in place, although some softening of the ration limits was gradually introduced. Unfortunately for consumers, the Ministry of Food announced that there was a growing tendency for traders to ignore the controls. The thinking was simply that the war was over, so there was no real need to take the controls too seriously anymore.

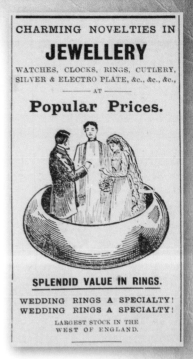

CHARMING NOVELTIES IN
JEWELLERY
WATCHES, CLOCKS, RINGS, CUTLERY, SILVER & ELECTRO PLATE, &c., &c.,
— AT —
Popular Prices.

SPLENDID VALUE IN RINGS.

WEDDING RINGS A SPECIALTY!
WEDDING RINGS A SPECIALTY!
LARGEST STOCK IN THE WEST OF ENGLAND.

Shops offer 'splendid value' to help romance along a bit.

A Glimmer of Light

Gradually circumstances did improve in many areas. As 1919 got under way, limits on meat changed for the better, with the value of a meat coupon extending to 5*d*, and certain meats – pork, poultry and game – being sold without need for coupons at all. However, things weren't always straightforward, with the situation relating to bacon in Swindon revealing some of the oddities in prices and quality at that time. One of the reasons coupons were lifted on the sale/purchase of bacon was that some butchers were actually selling their meat cheaper than the controls suggested: the control price was a maximum of 2*s* 4*d* per pound, while it was actually possible to buy bacon in the town for as little as 1*s* 8*d*. Confusingly, prices were not always an indication of quality. In some places bacon was of such an appalling quality that people refused to buy it even when they were tied to that particular supplier. This led to requests for friends to buy bacon from their suppliers instead, particularly since the poorer quality meat was often being sold at higher prices.

THE SWINDON RIOTS

On the evening of Monday, 21 July 1918, as celebrations were starting to wind down, murmurings of discontent filtered through the town, relating to the council's decision-making process around an expensive flagpole. Soon, large crowds gathered around the flagpole. Initially, they sang and shouted in good humour but as the evening wore on things turned sour. Tank instructor William George Blake witnessed it all and reported that 'a group of militants began to get out of hand'.

Despite the mayor and the director of the local theatre making attempts to pacify the angry men, their efforts were soon drowned out by calls to 'Cut the rope!' of the flag, followed shortly after by shouts to burn down the whole flagpole. By now, the crowd had turned into an angry mob, and the fire brigade and police decided to stand back rather than stir up more difficulties. Within minutes the base of the flagpole was burnt through, sending it crashing to the ground. Lifting the pole onto their shoulders, with the end still burning, a group of men led the crowd through the town, down Regent Street and Bridge Street, singing the whole way: 'Old soldiers never die, they only fade away!'

History records two different views of the riots, with the 'official' version differing somewhat from an ex-serviceman's point of view. Bavin, who worked for Swindon Council, reports that: 'There is nothing that reflects discredit upon the authorities of the Town or upon the great body of its citizens.' He then describes 'a small section that was not in sympathy with the Peace Celebrations … who are ready for any excuse to break into rowdyism', and suggests that the riots happening in Luton over that same weekend had planted this 'baser' idea in their heads. However, Blake, who of course had seen considerable action in the army, describes the scene of thousands of men marching and singing as 'very moving and emotional' and one he would never forget, making him feel that they were expressing the enormous pent-up feelings of four long years.

A faded picture of the charred flagpole (diagonally across picture) is all that is left to show of the riots.

On 16 December 1918, ninety-nine 'de-mobbed' horses were sold at Swindon cattle market, at prices ranging from 10 to 49 guineas per animal. More horse sales were expected, as 'remount depots' needed to be cleared, and many more horses were soon expected to arrive back from France.

Inevitably, lifting of price limits did lead to some blatant examples of profiteering, such as the price of eggs locally, and the ripping off of servicemen at the New Town railway station buffet. Here, men were expected to pay 4*d* for an orange, a price so high above the norm that the Food Control Committee issued a stern protest to the station manager. Later in the year, in August 1919, similar profiteering was responded to in strong terms by the women of the Vegetable Products Committee. The committee, in one of their last acts, rallied to the call on hearing that: 'Soldiers and sailors were victimised at the ports by cowardly knaves, without patriotism or generosity, who only sought to make a fortune out of their ignorance or necessities.' As a result, the ladies collected 2,600 large, healthy cabbages to be sent to the men of the minesweepers, with each vegetable weighing 6/7 pounds. At their final meeting on 3 November, the women's efforts over the war were totted up to reveal that they had sent some 324 tons of fruit and vegetables to the navy, with a total value of £9,072. This placed Swindon in third place out of 845 such groups across the country, with it also having the honour of sending the very last batch – twenty-five bushels of apples from Miss M.E. Story-Maskelyne of Purton.

Despite inevitable glitches, things generally continued to settle as 1919 progressed. In fact, as early as January, Swindon's Food Controller predicted that when current ration books ran out in May, no replacements would be issued. Perhaps unsurprisingly, things turned out not to be quite so simple. By May, it was true that most ration limits had been lifted after a carefully phased timetable, but purchasing restrictions on butcher's meat, butter and sugar were still kept. Through May, more relaxation took place with restrictions on jam lifted, although the maximum price remained, and, on 1 June, there was good news for retailers but not such good news for children, when the maximum price for sweets and chocolates was removed.

Finally, on 30 April, the local food control officer, Mr W.H. Bagnall, resigned from his position, with it clear that the role would soon be redundant.

Rebuilding

As the year went on, more limits were lifted, including those on the sale of alcohol. But it was not all good news: rationing still applied to coal, one of the biggest single costs in the family budget. The ration limit was even reduced for a while, despite the fact that the prices were so high no one could afford to buy much anyway. By November 1919, coal, often of an inferior quality, was selling at anything up to 52s 6d per ton compared to 19s per ton in 1914. Gas prices also rose, up to 5s 3d per 1,000 cubic feet, compared to 3s 6d at the beginning of the war. At around the same time, the council announced that water rates were to be increased by a colossal 30 per cent. After a very dry summer, and with the town still supplying water out to places like Chiseldon Camp, water was at an all-time low, and the council struggled to supply the town. Things got worse in September when the town suffered a strike at the railways, and water that was normally pumped into the town via the GWR's pipes from Kemble dried up. Fortunately, the strike came to an end, and the council found an extra supply from Poughcombe.

A soldier's work is never done – troops were employed in the rebuilding of the town and here are laying tram lines in Bridge Street.

The year also saw the realisation that the town was suffering a housing crisis. At the time this caused some confusion, with people drawing the simplified conclusion that 'For four and a half years hundreds of thousands of our young men have been killed; the houses we had before the war are still standing; there should be houses to spare instead of a shortage'. But this was flawed logic. The widows and children of those men were still in those houses, and the young had continued to grow up and get married. Most crucially, the war had all but halted the building of new houses. For four and a half years, the town's infrastructure had remained static. In 1914, Swindon had 12,729 houses, with an average of 4.4 people per house and a growing population – the average birth rate for the previous year was 23.39 per 1,000, compared to an average death rate of 12.08 per 1,000. By the end of the war, the population had grown to such an extent that competition in house-buying forced prices up to ludicrous highs. A house worth £400 before the war, was now selling for more than £700. In some cases the price rise was even greater. One row of houses, started before the war, were intended to be sold at £550 each. By the time building work was resumed in 1919 the houses were selling for up to £1,100. For many, this sort of cost was well beyond their means. The town's women decided to take action:

Women's Section of the Swindon Labour League – resolution to Town Council and Local Government Board – Nov 1918:

That this conference of representative residents of Swindon, believing the good housing of the people to be an urgent social reform, demands that the Government take immediate steps to compel local authorities to provide adequate housing schemes to be financed out of public funds, in order to provide the houses needed at the end of the war; but that no private enterprise shall receive public money for such a purpose; and that no building materials be released for the construction of such luxury-buildings as hotels and restaurants until the demand for adequate housing schemes has been met.

Furthermore, in an example of how things had shifted between the sexes during the war, the women demanded that they should be consulted at every stage of development. Even so, when plans for new houses were developed, the prices were far higher than anyone expected. The Swindon Labour Party objected in the strongest terms upon discovering that new houses were to be built costing anything between £774 5s and £1,020 5s. By the time costs for roads, sewers, etc., were added in, the average price was more like £1,100 per house.

Nonetheless, house building did start again, and industry started to pick up too. The years after the war were generally not good across the country, but Swindon did not suffer as much as many places. This was partly due to the GWR inevitably, but unemployment figures (mostly composed of numbers of ex-servicemen) were brought down by other industries too. Three factories that had been taken over for war efforts attracted Messrs Garrard & Co. down from London to make small motors and fine tools; Wills reopened their tobacco factory; and a new company took over Compton's clothing factory on County Road.

In tandem with the physical and industrial growth, local 'systems' began to return to pre-war conditions. For example, the post office switched back to longer opening hours to allow for the increased number of men wanting to use the service before or after work. They also increased deliveries from two to three a day. And in the council, proper full elections were held again for the first time in many years, with another sign of change being the voting in of Swindon's first female councillor – Mrs Noble.

A Sense of Fun

Perhaps the best signs of a world restored came in the form of the resurgence of entertainments. For Swindon, the real benchmark that things were settling down was the reinstatement of the 'Trip'. Once a year, the GWR effectively shut down its Works and arranged for all of its employees to take special trains on a holiday to the coast, to places such as Weston-Super-Mare, Tenby or Weymouth. The frequent invasion of thousands of workers, all in the Sunday-best, for a week in July even led to St Ives being known affectionately as Swindon-by-the-Sea.

Some Swindon men inevitably ended up working with railways during the war. Second Corpal Charles Knapp served with 20th Broad Gauge Railway Operating Company Royal Engineers. He was killed in action on 16 April 1918, the only service man of this unit to be killed in action.

Of course, this event was not much fun for non-GWR Swindonians, particularly since many shopkeepers had to shut down due to the lack of trade it caused. Nonetheless, the fact that it was back was still a real sign of improvement.

In other areas, things returned to normal too. For example, the Swindon Town Cricket Club started playing again after a ceremony with the mayor on 24 March 1919, and with the club ground's landlords, the Goddards, kindly offering three rent-free years to help the club get back on its feet. In August, the GWR park on Faringdon Road saw another return, with the revival of the 'Juvenile Fete', a special event for the children of the town named that year as a 'Victory Fete'. Also in August, Swindon's 'most beautiful' event came back in the form of the annual Flower Show in Town Gardens – an 'unspeakable pleasure'.

The GWR park on Faringdon Road saw a 'Victory Fete', which filled the park to overflowing.

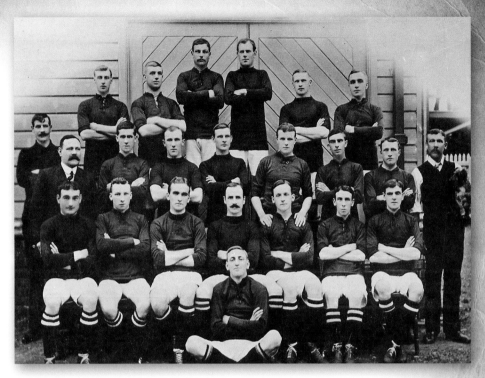

Swindon Town Football Team before the war with Freddie Wheatcroft (third from left on front row).

To many people, especially the men, one of the most important signs that things were getting back to normal was the 're-invigoration' of Swindon Town Football Club. Although the club had continued through the war years it was, of course, not at anything like the same level. Since the suspension of league games in 1915, Swindon had no professional players, a shortage of men (both players and crowd alike), and an interrupted, sporadic timetable throughout the war, often playing against military teams including the local Wiltshire Regiment. The 1919 season got off to a good start, financially at least, with a strong group of shareholders and directors and a very healthy bank balance of £957 5s 7d. The team didn't do quite so well. Before the war, Swindon had regularly triumphed in the FA Cup, and were Southern League champions in 1911 and 1914. Part of the team's success was down to Harold Fleming, a local celebrity who scored over 200 goals for Swindon in 332 matches, and was also capped eleven times for England. Sadly, Fleming had moved on by the end of the war, and it was quite a few years before Swindon Town started to show the same form again.

Even as Swindon Town started to rebuild its football fortunes, the memories of the war were never far away. Like every other area of life, the team had its share of tragedy. One of the team's prolific former centre-forwards, and England amateur, Lieutenant Frederick Wheatcroft, was killed in action at Cambrai on 26 November 1917, aged 35 (*see* Chapter 7: Moonrakers Across the World). A memorial erected in his honour reads:

> He played the game for his Town and he also played the game for his country and in that greatest of all duels, he fought for his country and, along with countless thousands, paid the Supreme Sacrifice.

POSTSCRIPT

LEGACY

The war between the Central Powers and the Allies finally came to an end on 28 June 1919, when, after six months of negotiations, a formal peace treaty was signed (the Treaty of Versailles). The treaty marked exactly five years since the death of Archduke Franz Ferdinand, the event that had sparked the whole terrible affair and led to over 16 million deaths and injuries to 20 million more. Such statistics are hard to comprehend, and, even now, vary hugely from source to source. Nonetheless, given the difficulties of recording facts during such a conflict, and the vast numbers of people who simply vanished (some estimates put this figure at 6 million), it is fair to assume the overall casualty lists are at the higher end of most estimates, which suggest a figure of 37 million casualties worldwide. Of these, 16 million died with approximately 10 million being military personnel; of these nearly two-thirds were lost in military action and a third due to disease (including the Spanish Flu). In the final analysis, calculations put over 6 million military deaths on the Allies' side, and 4 million to the Central Powers.

Beyond the military deaths, it is estimated that over 6 million civilian non-combatants died. Some of these deaths were a direct result of military action, but the majority were due to other negative consequences of the war, such as disease and malnutrition caused by the breaking down of hygiene, medical and food supply infrastructure.

For Britain, there were 886,939 lives lost in military service, plus 2,000 civilians. Over 100,000 other civilians were estimated to have

After the war ex-soldiers could join the Comrades of the Great War, a social organisation which was a pre-runner to the British Legion. Alfred Jerram was an Aldbourne man.

died through war-related accidents, famine or disease, bringing the total number of deaths to just under 1 million, with a further 1,663,435 military wounded. Measured against the population of the United Kingdom at the time, which was 45.4 million, the number of deaths meant that 2.19 per cent of the overall population were lost.

Town and Village

In Swindon, the rolls at the end of the war registered 920 men killed. However, since then, research has revealed several hundred more men, some who died after the end of the war, and with the figures complicated by what is meant by 'from Swindon'. Because of the difficulties of a fairly transient population, with some people being new to the town in the war years (coming to work for the GWR from, for example, Wales) and some living elsewhere when hostilities began, no one will ever know how many men from Swindon set off to war and never came home. A large plaque in the town hall carries the names of all those 920 identified at the end of the war, but current estimates put the actual figure at something nearer 1,300 men, who either lived in or were originally from Swindon, lost in military action. From a population of about 60,000, this amounts to about 2.3 per cent of the town's population lost, similar to the national average. But this is not the whole story by any means.

One of many memorial rolls of honour that were established around Swindon, this one in St Mark's church.

Firstly, that population figure includes women, children and older men as well as those of serving age. In 1915 the total number of men across England who were of military serving age was approximately 5.5 million, about 12 per cent of the population. On that basis, Swindon's 1,300 war dead account for more than 20 per cent of the male working population. In today's terms, this would mean some 5,000 men dying, from just one Wiltshire town.

Secondly, the figures make no account of those who lost limbs, or were otherwise incapacitated through wounds. Overall figures for those wounded suggest that half of those who saw action received an injury of some sort or another and, on top of that, war-induced illnesses took a huge toll, and we will never know the impact of what we now know as 'post-traumatic stress syndrome' on the countless men and women who witnessed the horrors of war through those five years. Countless men continued to suffer from shell shock, sickness and injuries, with many dying from wounds after the war had ended, and sadly, there are the silent figures of those who committed suicide.

And thirdly, the effects of the war did not go away overnight. In Swindon, one particular tragedy relating to the war shook the whole town. On Good Friday 1919, seven boys, part of a bigger group on an excursion to Liddington Castle (an Iron Age hill fort), wandered off in search of spent bullets on the ranges attached to Chiseldon Camp. One of the boys found something resembling a 'rolling-pin' and, despite warnings from his friends, rolled the object into a training trench. The object was actually a trench-mortar shell and exploded on impact. Three of the boys were killed instantly and two others were seriously injured. The boys had all been attendees of the Wesleyan Central Mission Sunday School, and their funerals were attended by one of the biggest crowds the town had ever witnessed.

The real story is, of course, told in the individual tales. This book has mentioned a very tiny percentage of those who suffered, but the story of the Ford family, who lived in Stratton, gives some idea of how life could be affected at a family level. The Fords had four adult sons who served, two who died, and a fifth who was turned down for military service. The sons' histories paint a picture of the diversity of Swindon's contribution and demonstrate how the legacy was passed down through the generations:

- Francis John (known as Jack) was already serving in the Royal Navy before the war. He was married with two children and lived in Weymouth. Francis was serving on HMS *Good Hope* and was lost when the ship was sunk at Coronel in November 1914.
- George William was a farmer by trade, married with five children. He enlisted in the 5th Battalion Wiltshire Regiment and was sent to the Dardanelles on 30 June 1915. Serving with the rank of sergeant, he displayed many acts of courage, one which led to the awarding of the DCM (Distinguished Conduct Medal) on 10 August: 'For conspicuous gallantry near Chunnik Bar on sustaining rapid fire until severely wounded as the company advanced at a disadvantage.' He died of his wounds later that day. His widow received his DCM at Reading from Major General Western.
- Herbert Charles had served in the South African wars with the Wiltshire Regiment and, after leaving the army in 1910, he emigrated to New Zealand. In 1914 he join the NZ forces and was made a training sergeant. He was sent to the UK before going to France where he was wounded in the foot. Herbert was later honourably discharged and returned to New Zealand.
- Archie Edgar served with the Royal Engineers on the Western Front and returned safely. He was married with four children and worked in the GWR till his death in 1943.

In Swindon's case, the tales of the other nearby towns and villages are as telling as those from Swindon itself, partly because of the close-knit nature of these smaller communities. Two neighbouring villages just east of Swindon present a powerful image of the impact of war on such places: Bishopstone (not to be confused with another Wiltshire village with the same name, south-west of Salisbury) and Little Hinton (also known as Hinton Parva, a name shared by a village in Dorset). Using memorial and thanksgiving plaques in the local churches, and research elsewhere, the local community has discovered that eighty-eight men from the village served during the war. Bishopstone sent fifty-nine men, from a male population of 235, and nineteen of

Two senior men of the GWR Works were given awards in the birthday honours list of 1918, specifically relating to their contribution to munitions production: George Jackson Churchward was made a CBE, and Charles Collett an OBE.

them died. Little Hinton's male population was 127, with the village sending twenty-nine men to fight, seven of whom died. The average age of the men in 1914 was 25 years and 4 months and at least 70 per cent of them were single (though six were known to have married during the course of the war). And, just as a footnote to the tragedy of war, there does not seem to be any record of six of the men mentioned on the memorial plaques. George Hawkins, Thos. Hawkins, Wm Meader, F. Archer, F. Griffen, and E. Watkins have, quite literally, disappeared off the record.

Remembering the Fallen

Although the struggle to regain a normal life dominated Swindon in the years immediately following the war, it goes without saying that the town was also passionate about its commitment to hon-ouring all those who had fought and died to save that way of life. Swindon had a temporary wooden memorial built, followed by a permanent stone cenotaph. Also, around the town and in the surrounding area, a huge number of memorial plaques appeared in schools, factories, village greens, different shops of the GWR Works, the town hall, and of course, the town centre. In most cases, the memorials were funded, or even constructed, by com-rades of the fallen. Earnest Culling, for example, fought in the

Crowds gather for the official blessing of Swindon's town centre memorial to the fallen, the Cenotaph.

war and later became a foreman in 'R' Shop at the GWR Works, where he took on the responsibility for collecting funds for the roll of honour for 'R' shop. Culling signed up for the Royal Engineers at the start of the war and, as part of 565 Troop RE (the Wiltshire Fortress Engineers), was one of those engaged in the building of the huge bridge across the Canal du Nord near Havrincourt. He won the Military Medal during the war but became very anti-war afterwards, not wearing his medals and refusing to take part in the Home Guard in the Second World War, saying he would never again wear khaki. Everywhere, men like Culling made sure their comrades were remembered and, in many cases, the memorials are still there today.

In Swindon, as in many other places, it is not only memorials to the men, but in some cases the men themselves came back to rest in peace on home ground. Many of Swindon's Great War dead are buried in the town's cemetery on Radnor Street, where, to this day, remembrance services are still held. The cemetery, created by Philips & Powell and George Wiltshire for £5,390 10s in August 1881, is a Commonwealth War Graves

The chapel at Radnor Street Commonwealth War Graves Commission cemetery.

Unveiling of 'R' shop memorial in the GWR Works, funded by the workers under the lead of R. Culling.

Commission (CWGC) cemetery, with 104 graves from the two world wars. The majority of these (eighty) are from the Great War, including that of George Wilkinson, who died from wounds received in action at Ypres. Earnest Culling also later joined his comrades in the cemetery.

Keeping a Record

As mentioned in the Introduction, this book owes a great deal to William Bavin for the amazing resource he left Swindon in *Swindon's War Record*, his book commissioned by the council and recording Swindon's part in war at the time. William Dorling Bavin was born on 26 February 1871. Before moving to Swindon in 1897 to take up the role of principal at Swindon Pupil Teachers Centre, he had been educated at Lincoln University, Westminster Training College and London University. He then became a tutor at Westminster Training College (1893–95) and Pupil Teacher Instructor at

Bath Municipal Technical School (1895–97). He later became Principal of the Central Higher Elementary School, Swindon; was examiner for various educational authorities in Somerset and Wiltshire; held the role of president of the Swindon and North Wilts NUT; and contributed articles to various papers and magazines on educational subjects (methods of teaching) and literary subjects.

Today, people can still visit the graves of the fallen across the world. This cemetery is at the battlefield of Arras.

Swindon's War Record was published in 1922, and draws much of its detail from local sources (including the newspapers and council records, etc.). It is a unique and invaluable reference for many aspects of Swindon and the Great War.

A New Generation

In the first month of the war, August 1914, H.G. Wells wrote a series of newspaper articles that were published collectively

Stained-glass window in the GWR Technical School, dedicated to forty-four of its students who were lost.